More Words

Gael Turnbull on Poets and Poetry

edited by
Jill Turnbull & Hamish Whyte

Shearsman Books
*in association with
Mariscat Press*

This first edition published in the United Kingdom in 2012 by
Shearsman Books Ltd
50 Westons Hill Drive, Emersons Green, BRISTOL BS16 7DF
in association with Mariscat Press, 10 Bell Place, Edinburgh EH3 5HT

Shearsman Books Ltd Registered Office 30–31 St. James Place, Mangotsfield, Bristol BS16 9JB
(this address not for correspondence)

ISBN 978-1-84861-093-4

Copyright © The Estate of Gael Turnbull, 2012
Introduction copyright © Jill Turnbull, 2012
All rights reserved.

Acknowledgements
Versions of some of these pieces previously appeared in *Agenda, Chanticleer, Chapman, Combustion, Compact, Credences, The English Intelligencer, Grosseteste Review, Kulchur, Lines Review, Mica, The Nation, New Measure, Northern Review, Northward Journal, PN Review, Satis, Scottish Poetry Library Newsletter, Scripsi, Southfields.*
'The Poet as Makar' previously appeared in *The Star You Steer By: Basil Bunting and British Modernism*, edited by James McGonigal and Richard Price (Amsterdam & Atlanta, GA: Editions Rodopi, B.V. 2000).
'Some Afterwords' previously appeared in *While Breath Persist*
(Erin, ONT: The Porcupine's Quill, Inc. 1992).

Thanks to Thomas Meyer, for the Estate of Jonathan Williams, for permission to reproduce a photograph by Jonathan Williams. Copyright in all photographs reproduced here remains with the photographers or their Estates.

Thanks are due to the following publishers for granting permissions
to reprint copyright material:
Bloodaxe Books, Tarset, Northumberland, for permission to quote from poems by Basil Bunting in *Complete Poems*, edited by Richard Caddel
(Tarset: Bloodaxe Books 2000).

New Directions Publishing Corporation, New York, NY, for permission to quote from poems by Robert Duncan in *Selected Poems*, edited by Robert J. Bertholf (1987; revised and enlarged edition, 1997), in *The Opening of the Field* (1960) and in *Roots and Branches* (1964); and for permission to quote from the following books by William Carlos Williams: *In the American Grain* (1933); *Selected Poems* (1985); *The Autobiography of William Carlos Williams* (1951); *The Collected Poems: Volume I, 1909-1939* (1986); *The Collected Poems Volume II 1939-1962* (1988).

Carcanet Press, Manchester, which holds the UK and Commonwealth rights, for permission to quote from *The Collected Poems: Volume I, 1909-1939* and *The Collected Poems Volume II 1939-1962* by William Carlos Williams.

GAEL TURNBULL (1928-2004) was born in Edinburgh, but grew up in Jarrow and in Blackpool, before emigrating to Winnipeg at the outbreak of the war with his father and mother, respectively a Scottish Baptist Minister and an American of Swedish descent. He returned to England in 1944 to complete his schooling and then to study Natural Sciences at Cambridge University. After rejoining his family in North America, he studied for an MD at the University of Pennsylvania and in 1952 became a GP and anaesthetist in northern Ontario, as well as providing medical assistance at logging camps in the area. There followed a short stay in London (1955-56), and a position as anaesthetist in Worcester until 1958, followed by a similar position in California. He returned to Worcester in 1964, to avoid the possibility of being sent to Vietnam as a medical orderly. He was to work as a general practitioner and anaesthetist until his retirement in 1989, whereupon he returned to live in Edinburgh.

An independent figure, he was central to the early transatlantic poetic contacts which were to have a transforming effect on many poets in Britain in the 1950s and 1960s. Frequently collected and anthologised, his own poetry was deeply personal and owed little to any particular school, although it is fair to say that his admiration for the work of William Carlos Williams, another poet-doctor, never left him and was an early driving force behind the discovery, and the maturing, of his own poetic voice.

JILL TURNBULL is a glass historian, author of *The Scottish Glass Industry 1610-1750* (2001) and articles on glass and ceramics. Born in Gloucester in 1936, she married in 1956, spending the next 25 years as an Army wife and having three children. She qualified in social work at Bristol University in the early 1970s, practicing initially in the Cotswolds and then as a mental health social worker in Worcestershire. After the break-up of her first marriage, she met Gael Turnbull in 1981. They married in 1983 and moved to Edinburgh following his retirement. After completing a degree in the History of Design and the Visual Arts in 1992, she worked for two years at Edinburgh College of Art, before completing a doctorate in the Scottish History Department of the University of Edinburgh, where she remains an Honorary Research Fellow. Since Gael Turnbull's death she has been his literary executor.

HAMISH WHYTE was born in Renfrewshire in 1947. He worked as a librarian in Glasgow for many years, and also as a bibliographer. He has edited several anthologies, including *Mungo's Tongues: Glasgow Poems 1630-1990* and *An Arran Anthology*. He runs Mariscat Press and has published the poetry of Gael Turnbull, Edwin Morgan and many others. His own poetry has been published in various magazines, and his long poem *Window on the Garden* was published as a book jointly by Essence Press and Botanics Press in 2006. A new collection from Shoestring, *The Unswung Axe*, is due in 2012. He is an Honorary Research Fellow in the Department of Scottish Literature at Glasgow University. He now lives in Edinburgh.

Also available from Shearsman Books & from Mariscat Press:

There are words… Collected Poems of Gael Turnbull (Shearsman 2006)

Dividings (Mariscat 2004)

Contents

Introduction ... 7

I. Canada, the U.S.A. and Migrant
An Autobiographical Sketch ... 11
Charlotte Chapel, the Pittsburgh Draft Board
    and *Some Americans* ... 15
A Letter from Canada ... 21
Migrant — A Personal Account ... 24
An Announcement ... 27
Dancing for an Hour ... 29

II. Basil Bunting
Then is Now: Meeting Basil Bunting ... 41
A Visit to Basil Bunting ... 44
An Arlespenny ... 53
The Poet as Makar ... 61
The Spoils, a long poem by Basil Bunting ... 63
Bunting, Brigflatts and Margaret Greenbank ... 65

III. American & Canadian Poets
A Visit to William Carlos Williams, September, 1958 ... 77
A Gesture to Be Clean ... 82
From a Notebook: A Speculation ... 93
Il Miglior Fabbro ... 95
Some Notes on *The Maximus Poems* of Charles Olson ... 97
Cid Corman ... 100
Some Notes on the Poetry of Robert Duncan ... 103
Allen Ginsberg ... 109
Paris and Bill Burroughs ... 111
Laura Riding: First Awakenings ... 115
The Selected Poems of Raymond Souster ... 118
Saint-Denys-Garneau ... 120

IV British Poets
What Is Poetry *About*? ... 127
Identity and Ideology or What Happened to the Poem ... 138
Resonances & Speculations, upon Reading Roy Fisher's *City* ... 142
Some Notes on *The Ship's Orchestra* by Roy Fisher ... 149

Edinburgh, May 1963 — Ian Hamilton Finlay	152
Letter to *The English Intelligencer*	163
Arabic and Persian Poems by Omar Pound	165
Hugh Creighton Hill's *A Soundproof Gesture*	168
A Letter to Sylvia Price Turner	170
William Price Turner: An Appreciation	173
John Adlard: A Memoir and an Appreciation	176
Some Remarks on the Poems of Emily Pfeiffer	181
Some Afterwords	198
Sources	201

Introduction

Creating poetry was Gael's first love, but he also enjoyed thinking, talking and writing about it. He took great pleasure in corresponding with fellow poets, and would make a real effort to meet with those whose work he admired, like William Carlos Williams and Basil Bunting, often establishing life-long friendships. One of his great pleasures was to encourage new writers and to publish them in *Migrant* and later in his "minimal missives". Some, like Ian Hamilton Finlay, became well known, others such as Hugh Creighton Hill never achieved the recognition Gael thought they deserved.

There are always choices to be made, and the selection of items for inclusion in this book has been influenced by their importance to Gael himself, as well as for their wider interest. Some are related to his support for those he felt to be neglected, whether they were his contemporaries, like John Adlard, or Victorians such as Emily Pfeiffer. Some of the journal entries were not intended for publication but they do, I think, offer insights into individual characters at a moment in time. Some are very personal. Gael enjoyed a close relationship with Basil Bunting, and he was very touched by Basil's reunion with Peggy, in which he played a part. His description of those events[1] was found tucked into a folder of Basil's letters—only to be read after the deaths of those involved. Parts of that story are known, but only Gael knew the full truth. The style of the individual subjects varies as widely as the subjects themselves—from stream of consciousness jottings about Ginsberg to academic musings on the nature of poetry itself. Their variety—and sometimes their intensity—reflect the man.

This collection of notes, memories, journal entries, reviews, critiques and comments indicates the wide range of Gael's prose—whether published, personal or polemic—all of it reflecting on the poets and poetry that meant so much to him. I am most grateful to Tony Frazer, who is responsible for the footnotes in this volume (except where otherwise indicated), and to Jonathan Greene for alerting us to the existence of the photograph on page 74.

Jill Turnbull
Edinburgh, July 2012

---

[1] See 'Bunting, Brigflatts and Margaret Greenbank', page 65-74 of this volume.

Canada, the U.S.A. and Migrant

An Autobiographical Sketch

In the autumn of 1952, I had expected to have started a research project at the Babraham Institute of Animal Physiology just outside Cambridge. Instead, I was in the small town of Iroquois Falls in Northern Ontario doing General Practice. How this happened is not immediately relevant even as the unexpected shift in my life has been very relevant, indeed crucial.

Not that Canada was totally unfamiliar. I had lived from January 1940 until April 1944 in Winnipeg and had even briefly travelled on a Canadian passport. There was no separate Canadian citizenship at that time and any British subject if they happened to be living in Canada automatically received a Canadian one. I had also acquired a Canadian accent something of which still persists and undoubtedly shall.

I was in Canada again in the summer of 1949 to Snow Lake in Northern Manitoba and had hitch-hiked through Western and Northern Ontario, then south to Toronto. For the 100 miles between Longlac and Hearst, there was only one forest ranger post. A few years before, there had not even been a road.

I was recently married. Our eldest daughter was born in Iroquois Falls and I had my first experience of working as a family doctor. When I arrived, I discovered that the person I was replacing had been chiefly responsible for giving the anaesthetics for the resident general practitioner surgeon and it was assumed that I would do the same. I was too young and too ignorant to admit my ignorance so I did not refuse. By the end of the three years we were there, I had acquired some proficiency and without serious mishap. This chance also greatly affected the pattern of my later life.

I was also given the job of what was called the bush doctor. Iroquois Falls was, and may still be, a company town, owned by the Abitibi Power and Paper Company. The wood pulp for the paper mill was cut from several hundred square miles of forest just to the north and east of the town. For reasons that I never fully understood, it was thought important to have a doctor tour the half dozen or so camps during the winter.

This was partly for any immediate medical care, partly as some sort of guarantee that the company was not negligent in regard to health and hygiene standards. What I actually did was minimal and highly inefficient but gave me a glimpse of a pattern of traditional forestry which was rapidly disappearing with mechanization.

I saw men working waist deep in snow with hand saws and horses, loading the logs on to sledges with a "jammer" (a system of pulleys from a vertical frame) which were then heaped in the frozen river or on the lake to wait for the break up in the spring.

But most of my time was spent by the stove in one of the huts staring out at the ice and snow. I would be out for 2 to 4 days at a time by the end of which I was thoroughly bushed and unable to concentrate on anything. The forestry engineers who ran the operation were virtually all English-speaking and university educated. The men were mostly from northern Quebec. This was my first real encounter with French Canada. I am ashamed now to think of how intermittent was my effort to learn to speak and understand. However, I did manage enough for the practicalities of "bush doctoring": the sprains, bruises, minor cuts and ever-present and ever-varied *la grippe*.

In the spring of 1953, John Sutherland published five of my poems in *Northern Review*. Although I had had some poems accepted previously by Peter Russell of *Nine*, those never appeared so that the group in *Northern Review* were my first publication and I owe a great deal to the generosity and encouragement of John Sutherland and his wife.

Almost immediately after, I received a letter from Raymond Souster who had read them, asking to see poems for his magazine *Contact*. To Souster also and his suggestions and criticism and interest, I owe equally as much or more.

The effect of all this on the course of my writing was crucial. Chiefly, it must be said, because Souster put me in touch with Cid Corman and his magazine *Origin* and a group of young American poets, also being published in *Contact*. I found myself reading, often with puzzlement or frank antipathy, writers with ideas about the writing of poetry very different to those with which I had grown up.

Of Canadian poets, I was soon reading and in contact with Louis Dudek, Irving Layton, D.G. Jones, F.R. Scott and others. Dudek sent me the gift of a copy of the *Autobiography* of William Carlos Williams which made an enormous impression on me. There were occasional visits to Montreal and Toronto. I published other poems in various Canadian magazines. I helped to edit a little anthology of *New Canadian Poetry* which was published as an issue of the magazine *Artisan*, by Robert Cooper in England. I never corresponded with A.M. Klein but his 'The Rocking Chair' is part of my permanent sense of both Canada and what poetry is about.

From being a solitary and unpublished writer, I became in those three years part of a community of writers, largely if not exclusively Canadian. How much this distorted, how much it stimulated and developed my writing, is difficult to guess. But effect, it certainly had.

In parallel to this exclusively English-speaking and writing world was my encounter with that other and French-speaking Canada. This was given impetus by my experience in "the bush" although there was the largely French-speaking twin town of Ansonville as well as many French-speaking people in Iroquois Falls itself, where there was a thriving French theatre group. I made particular friends with a completely bilingual local teacher, Jean Beaupré. It is perhaps difficult to imagine now but there was very little contact then, even in Montreal, between the poets of the two languages in Canada. I had been told on more than one occasion not to waste my time and energy trying to make contact. However, F.R. Scott had published some translations of Anne Hébert.

By prowling bookshops and some personal contacts—chiefly Avi Boxer, then living in Montreal—I read and corresponded with Gilles Hénault, Roland Giguère, Jean-Guy Pilon and Anne Hébert. I spent some time trying to read and understand Alain Grandbois. Eventually, with the help of Beaupré, I published four little duplicated bilingual collections of poems by Hénault and Giguère, and also by Saint-Denys-Garneau (by then dead) and a young Montreal poet with whom I failed to make personal contact but whose poems Avi Boxer had sent, Paul-Marie Lapointe. I was also struggling to read some contemporary French poets from France itself. Giguère himself was in Paris at the time.

I found the *Canadiens* most friendly and even patient with my dreadful schoolboy French on the few occasions that we met. For the translations of course I had Beaupré, sufficiently bilingual to correct and suggest idiom even in English. I became even more aware of the impossibilities of translation—and the fascination. But it was the poetry of Saint-Denys-Garneau which made the most enduring impression. This was not so much for the content of it—too introspective for my own use—but for a certain tone and pace of expression, where playfulness and gentle self-mockery shifted back and forth easily with great simplicity and vigour of expression.

It *is* possible—and I find myself hearing Saint-Denys-Garneau: "Il se peut que nous soyons trompés exagèrement sur ce compte..."—that I have been able to use something from his poetry in a poem such as 'Black Spruce' although there are other influences, some merely part of the conventions of French poetry generally (the *poème-en-prose*).

The 'Seven Snapshots' were written in 1965, a decade later, and in retrospect. There were many other poems that I wrote in Canada, some on Canadian subjects, some published, but these are the only ones that have survived, with 'Riel' (reprinted elsewhere). There is also a 'Jeu' or 'Ballad' (verses on the sanitary arrangements of a logging camp) still occasionally recited but not totally appropriate to a literary journal.

'A Night Call' was written in 1957 and broadcast on the BBC.

Charlotte Chapel, the Pittsburgh Draft Board and *Some Americans* : A Personal Memoir

I hope there may he some interest in tracing the curious sequence of events which led to the General Editor of *PN Review* to write to me, a General Practitioner in Worcestershire: "Charles Tomlinson in his book *Some Americans*, refers continually to your services to him which he suggests were almost of an institutional nature."

The references are only two and brief at that. But they do help to explain how the book came to be written. The story goes back to a visiting American Evangelist in Scotland in 1914 and the peculiarities of American Selective Service Law in 1952.

My father grew up in Edinburgh. His parents were deeply religious and had connections at various times with Presbyterian, Episcopalian and Baptist Churches in the city. In 1914, at the age of thirteen, he became converted during an evangelical crusade. This was under the ministry of a visiting American Presbyterian, Wilbur Chapman, working in association with the well-known Scottish preacher, Alexander Whyte. Even then, my father had a premonition that he might some day go to America.

Shortly after this, with his parents, he came under the influence of Dr Graham Scroggie at Charlotte Chapel in Edinburgh where his father sang in the choir. From 1914 to 1921, he worked for a farm fertiliser and feed firm in Leith and, under Scroggie, began the systematic Bible and Theological study which continued for the rest of his life. He also saved every penny he could for his future education.

Largely because of Scroggie's influence, in 1922 he went to the Moody Bible Institute in Chicago where he was for two years, and then another year at the McCormick Theological Seminary. While at the Moody Bible Institute, he met another student who came from a Swedish farming community in Minnesota. After his return to Edinburgh they were married.

When I was born, in 1928, he was a student at the University, working for his M.A. and supporting my mother and me by working as a supply preacher on the weekends. When I was three, we moved to Jarrow where my father began his first full pastorate on Tyneside, in the depth of the depression.

Thus I grew up as the minister's son in a very transatlantic family, in which devotion, books, study and writing were an immediate part of everyday life. How my parents managed to support themselves (and me) through it all, I shall never understand. They marvelled at it themselves.

After years in Blackpool, then in Winnipeg and later at Cambridge, I was a medical student at the University of Pennsylvania, from 1947 to 1951. I had already been writing poetry for many years. There is the obvious connection of the University of Pennsylvania with Ezra Pound, Marianne Moore, H.D., and most significantly, with William Carlos Williams. In my own case, it was merely a coincidence of practical circumstance.

I was only aware of Pound, whom I had read at Cambridge. His little *Selected Poems* published by Faber towards the end of the war was, and still is, one of the most loved and thus formative books in my life.

It was still possible to browse in the stacks of the University Library. I read systematically through most of the contemporary poets on the shelves. I even tried to read William Carlos Williams. I must have known that he had been a medical student in the same building where I had, on a couple of occasions, arranged a poetry reading in the cellars. But it meant nothing to me at the time.

I encountered his Introduction to the *Collected Later Poems*. Though born in Scotland, and with a transatlantic accent, I identified myself as somehow English. His stance seemed to me to be aggressively anti-English. I was immediately put off. If that was his line then it obviously excluded me. I shut the book with a sense of irritation. Why drag nationality into poetry?

By the summer of 1952 I was in Pittsburgh. I expected to return to England later in the year, to the Babraham Institute of Animal Physiology just outside Cambridge. But the American Draft Board intervened. They sent me call-up papers. I even got as far as having to attend for physical examination. They presented me with a neat *fait accompli*. I became, that very month, a qualified doctor. But I could not be a doctor in the American Army unless I was an officer. I could not be an officer, unless I was an American citizen. But I was a British subject.

Charlotte Chapel, the Pittsburgh Draft Board and 'Some Americans'

They were, from their point of view, generous. If I signed for a five-year stint in the Regular Army, they would give me citizenship. Otherwise I would have to serve my two years as a "non-doctor" like any other draftee.

I had no wish to serve at all: certainly not in either circumstance. I had just married an American, thus perpetuating my transatlantic links. Almost literally, we took the next bus for Canada and Montreal.

The following spring my first poems were published in the Canadian magazine *Northern Review*. By then, I was working as a doctor in a small town in Northern Ontario. Shortly after their appearance, I got a friendly note from a Canadian poet, Raymond Souster. He was editing a duplicated magazine, *Contact*. This was deliberately named after an avant-garde magazine with which Williams had been associated in his younger days, and was already publishing many of the names later associated with *Black Mountain Review*. He put me in touch with the American poet Cid Corman, who had started the magazine *Origin* a year or so before. Souster owed a lot to Corman. But without Souster's friendship and ability to open doors and general awareness of what was going on in America, this piece would certainly never have been written.

While reading one of the early issues of *Origin* (Vol. VI, autumn 1952) I came across a poem by an as yet unknown young American poet which irritated me a great deal. It seemed to be written so perversely badly that I singled it out and complained about it to Corman, with whom I was then corresponding. It was 'The Question' by Robert Creeley. The grammatical construction appeared to be not merely eccentric or compressed, but virtually non-existent or deliberately barbarous. Corman wrote back to the effect: "Try again." I did. I gradually came to *hear* the poem in a way that I had never *heard* it before. It fascinated me even as I could not logically understand how it worked. There was also a music which I could not scan but which radiated delight. I continued to have reservations—as I still do—that, in Swift's words, "It shall pass for wondrous deep for no better reason than 'tis wondrous dark." At the same time, there was a *light* in it which cast an essential illumination beyond any ordinary grammatical logic.

About the same time, there were extracts from some of Creeley's letters in Souster's *Contact*. I ordered a copy of his first book, *Le*

Fou, from San Francisco and was greatly impressed. There was a compression, an energy, an invention... in a way that I had never previously encountered. I wrote then in my journal (about 1953 or 1954): "Creeley comes very close to having done what I would like to do—one is always conscious of the living man, in activity, in commonplace situations—yet the result is never commonplace..."

From Creeley, I went back to re-read Williams. The Canadian poet, Louis Dudek, gave me a copy of the *Autobiography.* Suddenly I came to understand his intense preoccupation with being American. What had seemed narrow at first encounter did not seem to be that any more. His sense and use of the local was not constricting but liberating. It is true, his way of articulating this was not always helpful for anyone outside his situation. But there was a necessary vehemence without which, I came to see, he could not have survived.

In parallel with this, I exchanged letters with Creeley and continued to correspond with Corman who savagely criticised my poems, often to excellent effect. Eventually I had poems in *Origin* and even in *Black Mountain Review.*

When I returned to England in 1955, I was excited and challenged by the energy of a whole world of poetry that no one here knew about or wanted to know. Or so it often seemed. In fact, I was far from being entirely alone. There was the almost forgotten editor and publisher in Liverpool, Robert Cooper, and his magazine *Artisan.* In 1952 he edited a little anthology of *Nine American Poets,* that included Creeley, Duncan, Blackburn, Levertov, Olson and Corman. There were George Fraser's soirées in London, in the winter of 1955-6, where I took Robert Duncan on one memorable occasion, and where the world of what was possible extended considerably beyond the limits of Oxford and Cambridge. There was W. Price Turner and *The Poet* in Glasgow. Even John Sankey's *The Window* in London. There was Allen Ginsberg on the Third Programme when he was still hardly known in America. I have a photograph of the Zukofskys taken on the Malvern Hills in the summer of 1957, looking no less improbable there than they managed to look anywhere else. And Basil Bunting at Throckley, where I called to see him in the winter of 1956, cheerfully amused that I should have supposed him long ago vanished into some Persian desert. And

Charlotte Chapel, the Pittsburgh Draft Board and 'Some Americans'

*from L to R: Louis, Celia & Paul Zukofsky with Gael Turnbull.
Photo by Jonnie Turnbull*

journeys up to Birmingham to visit Roy Fisher to lend him books and magazines, and to listen myself, where Paterson, New Jersey seemed a much nearer sort of place than London. And many others.

Perhaps it was some vestige of my father's evangelical spirit that persisted in me. I made efforts to circulate some of the books that had interested me. My efforts were not very determined and even less efficient. These were from Jargon, Divers Press and Origin Press, chiefly by Creeley and Olson but also the Canadian poet Irving Layton. I eventually published a Selected Poems by Robert Creeley called *The Whip*. This was from Worcester under the imprint of Migrant Books, in 1957. It did get a few brief notices. Most of my own copies were given away. The bulk were distributed in the United States by Jargon.

This was the era of the so-called Movement poets, with their emphasis on a return to more traditional forms. I could not feel at home in any other country but this. At the same time, I could feel no identity with most of what was published and broadcast in the well-known places.

Now, in 1981, I have difficulty feeling much common ground with most of the American and Canadian poets I tried to champion then. Some of it may have been an enthusiasm born out of deliberate reaction. But not all of it. I think I was right, then, in perceiving that Creeley's early poems achieved both music and a compression of form that so many writing in more traditional structures perhaps intended but failed to realize. Equally, I think I am right, now, in perceiving how it is often more difficult to achieve such effects in so-called open forms than in the sort of poetry that Williams and others with him often attacked.

But the texture of any era is always more diverse than any generalisation or even list would allow. There are no rules for the flow of imagination. Some time late in 1956, I read and was greatly impressed by a little pamphlet of poems published from of all unlikely places, Oxford. It even had an introduction by one of the Movement poets, Donald Davie. This was *The Necklace* by a name completely unknown to me, Charles Tomlinson.

I don't remember how I got his address. I wrote an enthusiastic letter of appreciation. Then, inevitably, I sent him a couple of pamphlets of my own poems. He wrote back. He was generous. But among other comments he thought that they often showed the harmful influence of the American poet William Carlos Williams. I trust that he will forgive me if I quote from a letter of that time. Perhaps there is something to the dictum that all letters should be burned as soon as answered: "I think it a mistaken course."

I replied with evangelical enthusiasm. I sent him copies of some of Williams's books, in particular, *The Desert Music* and *Journey to Love*. These much later poems of Williams had not been published here. Even the earlier work, only partially. There was good reason for Tomlinson's ignorance at the time.

Tomlinson immediately wrote back with perceptive comments and was soon corresponding with Williams himself.

The rest all followed and eventually, nearly twenty-five years later, a book, *Some Americans*. Which might have been written without Dr Graham Scroggie of Charlotte Chapel and the Pittsburgh Draft Board. But then, perhaps not.

A Letter from Canada

Dear *Chanticleer*,

In your second editorial you invite your readers to "…comment and criticise…" It is easy enough to indulge one's peeves, and only too boring (or exasperating) to read someone else's. But you make the invitation, and I can't resist the temptation to respond.

The first thing that strikes me is how the translations from the French (Prévert, Supervielle and Queneau) stand out from the other pieces. Of course, a translator can pick and choose, can take the best of a whole generation; thus greater interest in translations is probably only as it should be. But when I ask myself the question: "What current work out of Britain might one show the French that would command equal interest?", then I am unhappy. While reading the poetry in several current British magazines, I find very little that is not a rather weary echo of the styles and moods of the past. And I contrast this with the translations of work by contemporary French poets that were featured in a recent issue of *Poetry (Chicago)*. Without trying to judge the final quality of the poems (I read French very poorly), I was struck by the atmosphere of energy, of the will to invent, of the urge to add in some way to what had already been done. They were poets not easily satisfied, hard at work on their craft.

In the first issue of *Colonnade*—so admirable in so many ways—I read:

> "The character of our century seems by now to be sufficiently formed. It is surely time to consider whether the twilight in which we live may perhaps be the precursor not of dawn, but of night."

Then I read in a copy of *Golden Goose,* from San Francisco:

> "It's about time that readers (also poets) face the fact that this is the *second* half of our century—that the battles of 1912–1932 are won, the advances secured… The work of this second half has started; a lot there if anyone beyond the usual few would pay attention… And fiddling with cocktail poetics and the pedantry attendant thereupon, is no guidance. Poetic theories have meaning only when they form a constructive basis for either reading or writing."

Perhaps I read too much into the contrast. And I am not raising the question *per se* of the quality of the poetry in the two magazines I cite. What I would like to suggest is that a young poet, trying to learn his craft, is more likely to get benefit from the second point of view, than from the first. Thirty or even fifteen years ago, the young poet might go to London to find the stimulus of fresh ideas. Now—as I gather from some of the editorials—he is more likely to find word-splitting quibbles about Neo-Romanticism or Neo-Classicism or some other "Neo" variant of something probably done better decades ago. And he may wonder if a lot of energy isn't being spent on diagnosing the exact state of poetry that might be better spent on the uphill job of making new poems.

The second thing that strikes me as I read your last two issues, is the strength of the anti-American feeling that comes out in some of the reviews. Having grown up and been educated in both Britain and the States, perhaps I am unduly sensitive about this. And it is easy to understand the causes of such an antagonism. For better or worse, it exists. What disturbs me more, is the possibility that a disgust with McCarthyism, Mickey Spillane and radio advertising, etc., may obscure some of the real achievements of American culture. Most particularly, that achievement in poetry.

As Joseph Bennet pointed out in an excellent article in a recent issue of *Nine,* most of this poetry is not only generally unread but is unobtainable in the United Kingdom. William Carlos Williams, Wallace Stevens, Robert Frost, and Marianne Moore, among the older poets, are talents comparable in their originality and influence to Auden and Thomas. That they have never received equal recognition and study in Britain is a loss to British writers.

Pound, it is true, has been published, and in some quarters given the recognition he deserves. But I suspect that this is because he spent many of his most influential years in London, and not because of any general current of interest in American work. Would he have been equally recognised if he had done the same work in New York? And if not, why must the poetry of the English-speaking world be restricted by the accidents of physical geography?

Further, I am not aware of any collection of current American poetry that is available in Britain which can compare in generous scope with Kenneth Rexroth's *New British Poets,* published by New Directions in the United States. (I may be wrong about this. It is difficult to keep up with all publications. But I don't know of any such work.) Why should this be? Must the balance of the exchange be to the loss of the British? After reading some of the current little magazines, I don't think the gap is getting any smaller. It's ironic, but I understand that when *Horizon* closed down, it had more subscribers in the States than at home. I doubt if any American magazine can boast of such *pro rata* interest. Yet there are several of equally high quality.

Maybe this has been a querulous letter, and has wandered from the pages of your magazine. But in a good cause. For literature is not grown in a window-box, or under a tub. A familiarity with a wide range of literary ideas may not influence the output of the occasional poet of indelible genius, but it is certainly an indispensable manure for the mass of minor writers, on which the total vivacity of a culture must depend.

Of course, "he that is without sin, let him cast the first stone". There is much that might be said on the other side. And I would like to end with a quotation from a poem by William Carlos Williams:

> We forget sometimes that no matter what
> our quarrels we are the same brotherhood:
>   …our wealth
> is words. And when we go down to defeat,
> before the words, it is still within and
> the concern of, first, the brotherhood.

In the same cause—

                    Yours,
                    Gael Turnbull

Migrant — A Personal Account

I am very conscious of two earlier magazines. *Contact*—edited by Raymond Souster from Toronto—was an immensely important influence, both in regard to writers and type of material, and in regard to general *atmosphere*. There was also *Artisan*, edited by Robert Cooper from Liverpool. But both of these had come to an end when I returned to England from Canada in 1955.[1]

In the autumn of 1956, I moved from London to Worcester. That winter, I bought a small stock of Divers Press, Origin Press and Jargon books with the idea of publicising, and selling them in Britain—this was under the name of Migrant Books. W. Price Turner, who edited *The Poet* from Glasgow and had published many American and Canadian poets of the period, supplied me with a mailing list of not much over 100. I sent out a set of duplicated sheets advertising and "plugging" the books and authors. These included Charles Olson's *Maximus Poems* and Irving Layton's *The Improved Binoculars*. I don't have a copy of this circular and my memory is not reliable as to precisely which books were listed.

In retrospect, the effort seems rather naïve and I didn't get anything near the response I had hoped. But, with various personal contacts, probably a few dozen books actually circulated and got read.

In the summer of 1957, I published *The Whip*, a small volume of selected poems by Robert Creeley, who arranged and managed the printing for me on Mallorca with Mosen Alcover, who had printed the Divers Press books. There were 500 ordinary card cover copies and 100 hard cover. This was still under the name of Migrant Books. It was intended to have been distributed in Canada by Contact Press, though I doubt if they ever handled very many. The bulk of the edition went out through Jargon—Jonathan Williams—in the United States. I did have the intention of publishing Olson's *O'Ryan Poems* but it didn't get further than "an intention" because I never got myself together enough to actually approach a printer in Worcester.

The first issue of the magazine *Migrant* appeared in 1959. It was produced on a hand-operated Sears Roebuck duplicator; there was

---

[1] See Jim Burns, 'Migrant Press,' *The Private Library*, Second Series, VI, I (Spring 1973), pp. 29-35 for an account and a checklist of the press; and *Poetry Information*, No. 17 (Summer 1977), pp. 95-98 for an index of *Migrant* magazine.

a simple printed card cover. The stencils were typed on a borrowed electric typewriter and I did approximately 200 copies each issue. The result was often scruffy but (usually) legible.

I decided that it was irrelevant to waste any time over subscriptions and sales and ran it on a give-away basis to anyone interested. Most people made a donation to help with postage costs. It came out with surprising promptness every two months for eight issues, the last an extra large double issue. I think it did achieve, because of this, a year and a half of continuity and concentrated impetus not usual in a little magazine. The readers and contributors ranged very freely across Britain, Canada and the United States, and in variety from Hugh Kenner in Santa Barbara to a chance acquaintance who ran a launderette in Worcester.

There is no doubt that I was more interested in what might be done with the British end of it. I felt exiled in Ventura and it was a way of keeping something going for myself, in contact with poets in both England and Scotland. I was also wanting to create a context that was not narrowly national and in which I felt I might be able to exist as a writer myself. In both of these concerns—though they may appear slightly contradictory—I feel I succeeded.

Michael Shayer provided an address and base in Worcester and was an active contributing editor. The final decisions were mine even as there were many things which reflected his particular concerns and the magazine would never have happened at all without his commitment. The use of anonymous material was important. I had the idea that it would provide a background which would give dimension and context to the formal poetry and prose. I can't pretend that this was completely original in concept but I do think that *Migrant* was distinctive in the way it was emphasized and in the particular slant of personal material.

With the eighth issue both Michael Shayer and I were confident that the magazine had fulfilled its usefulness at least for us. But its existence had attracted other writers, many of whom were completely unknown to us when we started. So we began to publish some pamphlet collections. Again, this was largely on a give-away basis, to interested readers, at minimal cost. Rather to our surprise, one proved something of a success, and we had to do a second edition of Finlay's *The Dancers Inherit The Party*, though probably not much over 500 copies, all told.

When I returned to England in 1964, the scene had changed completely. It would be foolish to say that Migrant had nothing to do with it, even as one could make a long list of other factors which had contributed. In 1958 there were almost no little magazines or little presses likely to publish any of the writers we found interesting. By 1964, a lot was happening. Michael Shayer took over the major editorial interest and Roy Fisher joined us to provide a business address in Birmingham. By 1965, Fulcrum Press was active and a whole new generation of writers, editors and publishers had appeared in both Scotland and England. There was no longer anything that Migrant could do that others could not do as well, and usually a great deal better. *Few* by Pete Brown was the last publication in 1966.

It was our biggest in sheer size, and somewhere, somehow, 1000 copies vanished into the bookshops and presumably, into the hands of readers. But that was 1968, when there was something of a poetry boom in Britain. If any book epitomises 1966 for me, it is Pete Brown's *Few*. A vintage year.

Since then, there have been a number of scattered items published under the Migrant Press imprint, especially in the past two years, but this has been a very different sort of enterprise and without the particular thrust it had from 1956 to 1966, and not relevant to this account.

An Announcement

Dear Reader,

MIGRANT will be published irregularly. It will contain writings—poems, tales, comments, confessions, versions from other languages. It is intended personally. For it to pretend to be a "magazine" with a "public" would be absurd. There is no such public: as there is a public for magazines with Circulation Departments. What subscription rate could there be? And so, it will be sent to anyone who wishes to receive it. That is, to anyone interested to read it. Thus our ambition will be to have a minimal number of readers; but for those readers to be maximally interested.

In early issues it is expected to include work by Cid Corman, Robert Creeley, Pierre Delattre, Ed Dorn, Robert Duncan, Roy Fisher, Merle Hoyleman, Thomas Lundin, Charles Olson, Michael Shayer and Raymond Souster—among others,

It will be available from:

    1199 Church Street, Ventura, Calif., U.S.A.
and from:
    2 Camp Hill Road, Worcester, England.

In a time when "little magazines" spring up and disappear constantly, another such migrant may seem a kind of vanity. And, in a sense, it is. It is that vanity which believes a personal effort is far from without effect. That what you or I do, or write, can be of use.

What is important? Where is the center of contemporary consciousness? It lies in what I say to you, what you say to me. What is language for, if it isn't so that one man can speak to another? But what we each say may be very different. And the saying of it will never be so simple as to require no art.

And so, to take what courage and caution can be had from another writer in another age—John Ruskin:

> "I believe that failure (in any direction of human effort) is less frequently attributable to either insufficiency of means or impatience of labour, than to a confused understanding of the thing actually to be done; and therefore (while it is properly

More Words

a subject of ridicule and sometimes of blame) that men propose to themselves a perfection of any kind, which reason, temperately consulted, might have shown to be impossible with the means at their command, it is a more dangerous error to permit the consideration of means to interfere with our conception... We may always know what is right; but not always what is possible."

*

If you would like to receive MIGRANT just send a letter or postcard to either address listed above. A contribution, even a few stamps, will be helpful; but chiefly we are interested to know who wishes to be on our mailing list. Any manuscripts should be sent to the Ventura address.

Dancing for an Hour

In the very different world of 1960, there were no State subsidies for writers, magazines or little presses. Pamphlets, often minimally produced, circulated because there were editors and publishers who believed in the work, and because there were interested and equally committed readers. It was also a smaller world than now, by which I mean that there were fewer of us: those who wrote poems and/or read contemporaries' work. To that extent, it was easier.

Among these was the magazine *Migrant*, which ran for eight issues, one every two months, the last a double issue, from July 1959 to September 1960. I produced this, mostly legibly, using a hand-operated duplicator, from where I was then living and working: Ventura, California. It was sent to anyone interested to read it, although contributions of cash or stamps were welcomed. Each issue was of approximately 200 copies and eventually there was a basic core circulation of about that number, divided in rough proportion to population between the USA, Canada, England and Scotland, with a scattering elsewhere. Most readers were involved with writing, chiefly poetry, in various ways: as writers themselves, critics, other editors etc, plus various libraries.

Michael Shayer, then living in Worcester, England, had a crucial role, not easy to define, combining functions of co-editor, distributor, critic and supporter, instigator and sounding board. His address appeared with the Ventura address on all issues. Although I had final editorial responsibility, he was free to make decisions also, and his involvement increased as time went on. Thus it was, in effect, except for physical production and my presence in Ventura, published from both places equally.

More difficult to detail, but more important, was the particular imperative which occasioned it, and the eventual "focus". Inevitably this was more multiple than single but for this account I will ignore factors personal to myself and try to describe the main concern which I had in common with Shayer. We both, if in varying ways and to varying degrees, felt a strong sense of isolation in regard to what was being published in Britain. We were interested in and impressed by much American and Canadian contemporary writing, especially poetry. At the same time, we were not part of that world either.

The magazine provided an opportunity to create a context in which things might happen, encounters occur, ways of expression be explored, ideas expressed. There were the anonymous prose comments, sometimes but not always directly related to other items in the magazine, occasionally manufactured by myself, and not all of which I would have particularly endorsed. I was pleased to see Leon Bloy in the same issue with some of Ed Dorn's earliest poems, an article by Alan Brownjohn comparing poems by Larkin and Creeley beside anecdotes from a Worcester launderette, Mayakovsky in Scots setting off Hugh Kenner on William Carlos Williams setting off other items which, at this distance, I cannot imagine why I included. Attempted jokes don't wear well.

Yet, in retrospect, I am amazed how well we did succeed overall. This can be measured specifically in terms of the fact that between the first and last issue—merely sixteen months—we had made contact with, among other writers previously unknown to us, Matthew Mead, Anselm Hollo, then based in London, and Ian Hamilton Finlay, for all of whom we would soon publish first collections of poetry. Roy Fisher and Edwin Morgan we already knew slightly, in different ways, but the magazine helped us to focus our interest, and perhaps theirs, on what they were doing.

From surviving letters it is possible to reconstruct a sequence. Shayer wrote to me on 26 February 1960, after four issues had appeared: "…this will amuse you. I got just two poems, nothing else, out of the blue from one Finlay, from Edinburgh. I was foolish enough to commit myself on them (thinking, alas, he was [only a student]…) and saying that they seemed to have a traditional metre and rhythm etc. which prevented anything worthwhile being said—to have my balls chewed off by return for being patronising. And this indignant letter and four more poems included *may* be something for *Migrant*, after I've finished digesting them."

On 6 March, he advised me to add Finlay's name and address to the mailing list (significantly also, Anselm Hollo's) and wrote: "I find… from time to time, a fresh taste of what I have already looked at comes up… and then, all of a sudden, I find the mist blows away, and I can either reject confidently or say yes. The first thing I've said yes to are these poems of Finlay's. They seem to me to be absolutely genuine, and notice, by the way, the resonance between some of the gayer poems of Creeley's and this 'Clever Joan'.

Notice a singing, tough, very individual rhythm underneath them. They are closer to what the 'English' (note the sarcastic quotes) recognise by poetry. [Presumably by contrast with Creeley's.] I don't want to say too much about them… until you have seen them, and until I've been able to tell Finlay something of why I gave the thumbs-up… but I would suggest you printed 'Finlay's House', 'Optimist', 'Orkney Interior' and 'Island Moment' in *Migrant* 6, if you can find space, and 'Black Tomintoul' and 'Clever Joan' in 7. I think they are worth some prominence, rather than cramming the lot in the monster 7. And I wouldn't suggest you printed 'An Evening' at all."

In fact, with slight modification, groups of poems appeared in issues 7 and 8; and Shayer's letter then explains why he wasn't happy with 'An Evening', which, indeed, Finlay did not include in his selection for *The Dancers*. Shayer continues: "Also, I include a letter of [Finlay's], marked tentatively with the passages which I think could well be used anonymously in *Migrant*." This excerpt appeared in *Migrant 8*.

On 5 April 1960 Shayer remarks, presumably in reply to some response of mine, "Good, good, on Finlay and Mead", also giving me Mead's address. On 19 April: "Finlay has a new note, which I hope you're going to hear, both in letters and poems and plays (I mean, *I* have heard it). It *may* be—I haven't sorted this or MacDiarmid out yet—that Finlay has got what MacDiarmid only rants about.' In the same letter he remarks on an interesting letter from Edwin Morgan, probably the seeds of what became *Sovpoems*, and "I play around with the idea of putting… some of Fisher's Birmingham material into one issue." This later became *City*.

Migrant 6 (May 1960) listed Finlay among contributors to forthcoming issues, and he had already become enough of an accepted part of the context in which we saw ourselves that on 20 May Shayer remarked of "…Fisher, Finlay, Shayer, Turnbull etc."

On the back of an envelope postmarked 20 June 1960, Shayer wrote: "This, from Finlay, in reply to something I had said, in the post today…" followed by the text, in quotation marks, of the title poem to *The Dancers* but without a title, almost as if it had been a quotation from Finlay's letter. These lines begin, as he transcribed them:

> When I have talked for an hour I feel lousy
> —not so when I have danced for an hour
> The dancers inherit the party . . .

On 24 June, he wrote: "Firstly, Finlay wrote and asked, Would I like to do a lengthy group of poems of his as you have done the Dorn thing [the pamphlet, *What I See in The Maximus Poems*] to come out as a *Migrant* pamphlet, and I said, Nothing would give me greater pleasure at the moment. (We can discuss later whether you or I will do the printing of it)."

This is followed by information from Finlay about Castle Wynd Printers and his book *The Seabed,* and that there was a copy of this book already in the post for me.

I must have written to Finlay myself some time in April, and certainly there is an air letter from him, addressed "Dear Gael Turnbull", postmarked 2 May 1960, from his address in Northumberland Street. In it, he gives his permission to use the extract from his letter to Shayer, as already mentioned, and "I am glad you like the poems, of course."

The next extant letter is dated 8 July and mentions that he realises that I have not yet seen the whole manuscript of what became *The Dancers Inherit the Party*, and that "...nothing could be fairer than that you should see the poems you are going to publish. I'll have my selection if possible typed, and sent off to Michael: say he'll get them in two weeks from now at the latest, so then I'll wait to hear from you." He also gives the name and address of Zelyko Kujundzic, who would do the woodcuts for the cover and frontispiece, so that I could make the contact.

The final issue of *Migrant* (number 8, September 1960) gives advance notice of publication of the pamphlet, as "ready October 1960", with listing of the earlier pamphlets by Mead and Dorn, all at 1/6d or 25¢, stamps accepted. Finlay's name is given as "Ian H. Finlay", as this was how he then signed himself, had written on the manuscript and used for his *The Seabed and Other Stories*.

I was uncomfortable with this and in letters that summer discussing the manuscript and production details, I queried it, noting that there would be advantages in being more clearly distinguished from another Scottish author, Ian Finlay. I think I made the suggestion of I H Finlay, but he did not like that and on 19 September he wrote "About the name, yes, please use Ian Hamilton Finlay, I think I'd really be pleased."[1]

In the same letter he remarks: "I was very impressed by the copy of *Black Mountain Review:* what a smashing magazine." This was probably the one surviving extra copy I still had of one of the last issues, and probably his first introduction to that particular group of writers. Certainly his letter of February, from which the *Migrant* extract was taken, is careful to distinguish his Scottish experience from an English one but looks to "the Russians, the Germans, the Scandinavians" without any mention, specifically or generally, of Americans. But by 5 July 1961 he was writing of his sense of isolation in Scotland and about "…Creeley, Dorn, etc.—I feel they are my brothers."

On 9 November Finlay wrote to thank me for the airmail copy of *The Dancers*—which had just arrived. He noted two errors, the word "new" missed from the last line of 'Twice', and one comma missed in 'Orkney Lyrics', "…but that is like Life's inevitable income tax." Otherwise, he was delighted. Shayer received his stock, by surface mail, on 9 December, by which time others in Britain had already responded. Shayer quoted from a letter from Roy Fisher:

> Walked out to find Finlay's book lying despairingly on the doormat, too-large and stiff to go through the slit. An arrival fraught with omens.
> I think it's very good: a satisfying substantial object, and excellent poetry. The regional quality appears truthfully in Finlay, nothing precious about it, for he sees nowhere else he could be.

---

[1] Perhaps he had forgotten that he had already used this form in 1950, when an early poem of his was published in the American *Quarterly Review of Literature.* Curiously, in retrospect, this was in the same issue as part of a short novel by Louis Zukofsky, although he may not have registered that at the time. I did not myself stumble on a copy of the issue until later. [Author's Note.]

Shayer added that Fisher had further responded "…both to my invitation to do a B'ham poems pamphlet, and to Finlay's poems, by… wanting to write the book from scratch. Hurrah! Also, Edwin Morgan is on, I think."

Already, he requested more copies and by 23 December was reporting even more orders "…this makes 43 so far" and that "Morgan is going to review the pamphlet in a Glasgow paper [the *Glasgow Herald*]." Many readers, having received their own copy, ordered extra ones to pass on to friends.

In fact, it proved a best-seller, to the extent that it became apparent that the initial 200 or so copies would soon be exhausted so a second edition (slightly revised, of 300 copies) was planned, which appeared in the early summer of 1962. By then, some of the poems had been reprinted, thanks to Hugh Kenner, in America (in *The National Review*), and much later the entire collection was reprinted in a *New Directions* annual.

Finlay was not encouraging about review or complimentary copies in Scotland, except to known friends, and much regretted that I had sent one to MacDiarmid.

I certainly had a positive response to the copy I had sent to Robert Duncan although I can find no letter about this. Robert Creeley wrote from Guatemala where he was then living, on 2 February 1961, "Thank you very much for that book of Finlay… it's a lovely tone of wit and good nature which he proves…" In a later letter of 25 August, from Albuquerque, he remarks "…Finlay, the more read, the better."

Louis Zukofsky wrote, on 12 December 1960: "Thanks for Finlay—charming—he is a poet, it's about as simple as that—a Scots LORINE NIEDECKER who by the way would, I think, like his work very much if you can spare a copy—her address [is]…"

On 21 January 1961, he wrote—possibly in reply to a letter of mine to report that I had heard from her or was it he who had heard?— "I knew Lorine would fall for the Finlay, perhaps she wrote to you—or rather I think she said she did. And if the Russkies [*Sovpoems*], Finns (Anselm Hollo's pamphlet) and Fisher [*City*] are as good—good."

How the direct contact between them and Finlay eventually occurred, I don't know, but the essential link had been made, and probably first with Niedecker. On 26 June 1961, Finlay wrote

> If you could ever send me (find me) any Louis Zukofsky I would be very pleased. The more I see of American poems, etc., the more I feel they have arrived at much the same conceptions as I have, in my own wee way, rather home-made, and AGAINST everything I was taught to do by other Scotch writers. I think Lorine Niedecker's poems are superb. I am fair touched.

In a footnote to the same letter he remarks "I have just realised how *wonderful* Creeley is! Terrific", and on 5 July he wrote, amid much else, that "I had a man down last night, trying to get him to translate some Lorine Niedecker poems into Gaelic."

Cid Corman was sufficiently interested that by 5 July 1961 Finlay mentions sending his poems for *Origin* and eventually an issue appeared with an extensive selection of new poems, with extracts from letters.

There were, of course, many others. On 5 January 1961, Finlay wrote from Aberdeen: "There was a nice wee notice of the poems by E. Morgan in the *G. Herald.*"

One of the letters from Finlay postmarked 5 July 1961 but headed simply "Tuesday", mentions "I'd like to bring out a new collection of wee poems called *Whistling in the Dark*—but Lord knows who would do it."

Then there is a letter postmarked 6 July, headed "Thursday", which starts with a note by Finlay and revised text of a poem from the previous letter, followed by an additional and longer text, in a different hand, addressed "Dear Gael Turnbull". This ends "My address is Jessie McGuffie, 24 Fettes Row (2nd. Flat) Edinburgh. I send you all good wishes."

Her letter begins:

> I am intending to start publishing a series of wee books of poems to try and counteract the terrible depressing kind of writing that always gets published here in Edinburgh these days. I want the series to be non-provincial, but *Scotch* or *American* or *Wherever-from* art, looking all beautiful with linocuts too. It's to be called The Wild Hawthorn Press. Sorry. Forgot to say the first wee book is to be *Whistling in the Dark*—12 poems by Ian.

She then goes on to ask about use of the *Migrant* mailing list and to hope that I might be able to get a usable "quote" which could help to publicise it "from somebody like Robert Duncan or Creeley or somebody you know who likes Ian's poems". Morgan was perhaps too near, and in those days, not particularly well-known. *Sovpoems,* by then published, was only his third pamphlet.

I collected at least three such quotes from those who already had public reputations, at least in America. There may have been more.

From Robert Duncan: "Well, I'm landed, or taken in by them, and it's all another water of their own, and my own must skip sometimes to something of Finlay's tune."

From Robert Creeley: "There is in Ian Finlay's work such an ease of humour, and such pleasure of song, that wit follows—and a world likewise."

From Hugh Kenner: "He fishes no one's waters, and no one else can fish his, or even arrive at where they are. What would be whimsy from an Englishman, Finlay invests with bleak and casual panic, as though on the edge of the world."

By 14 August there were, from The Wild Hawthorn, in addition to the projected *Whistling in the Dark,* plans for books by Lorine Niedecker (*My Friend Tree*), Robert Garioch, translations of Attila József by Edwin Morgan, Karl Kraus—*Poets of the Cuban Revolution,* and an untitled "Poems/Prose" by Louis Zukofsky.

There was also: "Ready next week from The Wild Flounder Press, Dada of the Wild Hawthorn Press—*Glasgow Beasts, An A Burd*" and at the bottom of the letter "Now we have another hundred leaflets for Migrant Festival poetry readings to put out at once, so must stop." This was from Finlay. In a handwritten continuation, but on another air letter from the same day, "Monday", he apologises for being so busy and ends with

> In Rousay there's a lovely old mill for sale for £200—we could buy it, make stone-ground *real* flour, bag it in wee bags, and sell it to the English at posh prices. And one could turn one floor of the mill into a publishers: Migrant/Wild Hawthorn—what say you?

Sadly, that mill was not bought. It might well have proved a disaster but there are times when folly would have been much the wiser. It is difficult to understand from Finlay's surviving letters exactly what happened with the Migrant Festival poetry readings in Edinburgh that August. Certainly Shayer was there, Edwin Morgan, Anselm Hollo, and Michael Horovitz (presumably with his *New Departures)*, and Pete Brown, as there is mention of all of them. There were disasters with the first printing of *Glasgow Beasts* and battles with the printer to have it done properly. There were too many visitors at 24 Fettes Row, especially poets. There was Fionn Macolla in a state of crisis. There was the general obduracy of the world and thick-headedness, even deliberate perversity, of most of humanity, especially in Scotland. As indeed Shayer and I also had our harassments and distractions.

Nonetheless, the Wild Hawthorn continued to flower, if not quite as originally projected. *Whistling in the Dark* never appeared. *Migrant* also continued, if less consistently, by then transmuted into Migrant Press. But all that is outwith the span of this account.

One last swirl, as it were, of the dance, and which I would be sorry to think might slip into total oblivion.

In the summer of 1963, I made a visit to Scotland and England, arriving, by way of Reykjavik, at Prestwick. I had some copies of the second edition of *The Dancers* with me, and as I went through Customs, had to open my suitcase for inspection.

The Customs Officer obviously recognised them and Finlay's name, made some cheerful comment which I have forgotten, and waved me through. It was as if he were expecting them and me. It was only after I was settled on the bus on my way to my aunt's at Uddingston, that the unlikelihood of it came to me.

But then, perhaps, no more or less unlikely than any of it.

Gael Turnbull with Basil Bunting, 1968. Photographer unknown.

Basil Bunting

Then is Now: Meeting Basil Bunting

I wrote this in 1961 and it appeared in an American magazine as part of a longer prose piece. I should explain that part of my boyhood was spent in Jarrow and I was often there to stay with friends. Basil Bunting was then living in Throckley. He is not mentioned by name. In that, the piece expresses what is transitory in us, what is enduring in the poems. The incident occurred in the winter of 1956. I have not tried to revise it. When he read it years later and I had come to know him better, he was amused by the "image of a scoutmaster" and remarked, "That would be the Wing Commander Bunting!"

Nearly thirty years from that occasion and after his death, there is a sense in which very little has changed. "What he has written is on a shelf at my elbow. And as I read it here, now… what exists is here and now…"

Or, as he went on to write in 'Briggflatts', "Then is subsumed in Now."

The last time I was on Tyneside, I had in my notebook an address which I had obtained, quite by chance, in Canada. It was given to me as the address of a certain writer, a poet, whose work I greatly admire. A scribbled address, in an adjacent town—a street and a number—to which I went one day, on an impulse.

It was a place I had known as a person. This was a man I had known only through his writing. But the conjunction happened, as it sometimes happens; as, at some time and some place, it must happen.

Up a slanting street, with a view out over the valley of the Tyne. Up some high steps, to an ordinary door, any door. With a man to open the door, to say, "Yes, I am—" and to greet me. A little amused perhaps at my obvious surprise that he existed. How could it be? And how could it be otherwise?

My first bizarre reaction: how much he was my story-book image of a scoutmaster. Then, another image, of dignity and honour. Later, in conversation, he said of someone else, "There was no side to him." The slightly old-fashioned implication of "side"; and its enormously appropriate relevance.

We sat in the kitchen and talked. He spoke of his life and of the writing of poetry. Of the war and of his travels. Of Persia and Isfahan, of the wines of California, and of Los Angeles before the freeways came. Many places, many people.

He showed me a Koran, and translations from the Arabic, ornate and sinuous verse. Reading to me with a slight Northumberland accent, a roughness to the consonants.

More Words

> An arles, an arles for my hiring,
> O master of singers, an arlespenny!
>
> —Well sung singer, said Apollo
> but in this trade we pay no wages.[1]

Then, my surprise to discover that the accent in 'Samangan' came on the *gan;* and what a shift it made in the rhythm, as he read:

> Let them remember Samangan, the bridge and tower
> and rutted cobbles and the coppersmith's hammer,
> where we looked out from the walls to the marble mountains,
> ate and lay and were happy an hour and a night;
>
> so that the heart never rests from love of the city
> without lies or riches, whose old women
> straight as girls at the well are beautiful,
> its old men and its wineshops gay.
>
> Let them remember Samangan against usurers,
> cheats and cheapjacks, amongst boasters,
> hideous children of cautious marriages,
> those who drink in contempt of joy.
>
> Let them remember Samangan, remember
> they wept to remember the hour and go.[2]

We crossed the street after opening time, to a modern pub; quite a posh place, and still uncomfortably new. He drank double brandies, enjoying them easily, the good humour in his eyes deepening and becoming almost rakish. He told me of a Quaker upbringing, and of prison as a Pacifist in the first World War while he was still scarcely more than a boy.

Later I caught a bus to get home. Waving goodbye to him, standing there on the pavement, at the bus stop, at the very edge of the curb,

---

[1] This is the beginning of the untitled 12th poem in Bunting's *First Book of Odes*, in *Complete Poems* edited by Richard Caddel (Tarset: Bloodaxe Books 2000; New York: New Directions 2003).

[2] This is the complete text of the untitled 32nd poem in Bunting's *First Book of Odes*, in *Complete Poems*, op.cit.

under a street light, with the darkness all around. A little mist, to gentle the sight.

I have never seen him since. Though he is still there. As the houses are still there, and the drains, and the cemeteries, and the allotments with miles of cauliflower heads.

As what he has written is on a shelf at my elbow. And as I read it here, now… what exists is here and now…

A Visit to Basil Bunting[1]

*Gael Turnbull (left) with Basil Bunting at Wylam, Winter 1965.
Photo by Jonnie Turnbull*

Basil—reading his new poem to us, the first section, twice through—at my request—Mike and Tom and I sitting on the floor, Connie[2] in the chair with Matthew—"Let me know if it seems complete nonsense, won't you…". Explaining that the place where Eric Bloodaxe was ambushed and killed was not exactly on the route that the wagon with the headstone took, "But close enough. So that one is aware of it". The locale being Yorkshire and not Northumberland, a little to our first

---

[1] Dated *Winter '64/'65* in one of the author's notebooks.
[2] The Mike, Tom and Connie referred to in line 2 are Michael Shayer, Tom Pickard and Connie Pickard.

surprise. (But ancient Northumbria included Yorkshire.) Explaining there were to be two more sections—the next to deal with how the marble came from Carrara. Repeating again and again that there were stanzas that were all wrong, that he must re-write. Mike pointing out one—the curiously perfunctory *reportage* of it contrasting with the rest of the poem. But mostly we were silent. A little stunned. I said that one phrase about "words slip etc." seemed an uncomfortable echo of Eliot. He didn't seem bothered. "I'm sorry if it is. Of course, it's probably that we both thought of it. I used the sonata form, perfected it, almost the same time as he did." Reading from a small (4"x3") hard-cover notebook. The pages all squiggled and scratched, but part of it typed up on small sheets of cheap paper.

He was Ford Madox Ford's[3] "young man" for a few months, in the '20s, the ostensible job to help with the editing of *The Transatlantic Review*. He helped correct the proofs of the first book of the *Parade's End* sequence. Ford had had some sort of verbal tic, ending sentences with the same word. B. had crossed this out through the whole ms. At first FMF seemed upset. Then sat counting them, up to 40 or more. Then let B. finish. "I rewrote quite a lot of it. He seemed satisfied." But the job grew bit by bit, so that he was changing the baby's nappies and doing other household chores. Hemingway succeeded him.

One day Hemingway came to see them, reported that he had found a café with a supply of prewar Guinness. The 3 went. Finished every bottle. It took them 3 days of steady drinking. Going out for food at times in between.

Remembers Yeats in Italy, talking at a café with him and some others, "If the British public knew what we were saying they'd hang us all!" That Yeats was often with people, the conversation around him, and might not hear a word all evening, lost in some reverie. But if jogged would attend to a specific question or remark.

---

[3] Ford Madox Ford (originally Ford Hermann Hueffer, 1873-1939), novelist and essayist, and editor of *The English Review* and *The Transatlantic Review*. Today he is best remembered for his novels, *The Good Soldier* and the *Parade's End* tetralogy.

He met his first wife in Europe (American / rather admired D.H. Lawrence.) They got married in the States, his first visit. This must have been about 1930. "I spent $5 on the licence. $5 to pay the judge. And it cost us $5 to get back to New York. And then we were broke." They went to Margaret de Silver's apartment. She was, or had been, a millionaire heiress. (Was also nearly penniless when she died years later). Gave nearly all of it away, mostly to writers & artists. Had given Basil £200 a year for two years (roughly 1928-30). In the dedication to his first pamphlet—Milan 1930—he thanks her. "Saved me from journalism. In those two years, I had a chance to learn my craft."

When Eliot became editor of the *Criterion* he said to B, "No one should be an editor for more than 2 years." He stayed on for twenty.

When, in Paris in the '20s, Eliot declared himself a Royalist, an Anglican etc., B. says it was really all a sort of joke, just to be different. As time went by, he began to believe it.

Yeats had memorised one of B's poems, and used to recite it. The one about foam.

Eliot rejected 'Chomei'[4] (from the *Criterion*) on the grounds (says B.) that B. had never lived in Japan & didn't know any Japanese. "I might have done the same, if I'd been editor." The version is made from an Italian translation to be found in Italy. But despite this, he has had it from some Japanese that his version retains a remarkably fine sense of the original.

He picked up a book of translations, in Italian, from the Persian, in some bookshop on the coast. But it was defective, the last 1/3 missing. Pound bought & gave him (1) the complete original Persian text (2) a dictionary. He worked through it this way, without a grammar. He learned Italian the same method, using Dante; "the only way to really learn a language. Slow, but thorough. Piecing the grammar together yourself as you go." But when he went to Persia, in the war, as "an expert", he had never spoken a word or heard it spoken.

---

[4] 'Chomei at Toyama' (1932), one of Bunting's longer poems.

A Visit to Basil Bunting

He smokes heavily, especially when sitting talking, if not exactly a chain smoker. Has a shocking cough at times. The veins standing out in his neck & forehead. Slightly nicotine fingers. His moustache down hiding the upper lip altogether, somewhat yellowed, staining the grey. Bushy eyebrows, that curl upwards at the corners. (I remarked to him that I like the profile photo of him used for the Morden Tower Reading poster, but that it missed his "devil's eyebrows". He laughed & seemed to like this.) A lot of hair in his ears. Become a bit stooped & shuffling since my first seeing him in 1956. Rather more obviously only enjoying "old man's talk". Reminiscences of the past. Though brightening always at any mention of Tom Pickard.[5]

We talked until 2 a.m. or later. He showed me a poem he had done, 'A Song for Rustam'?[6] "It's wrong. It's wrong somewhere. I don't know where. Can you tell me what's wrong with it? There is something terribly wrong". And it was. The personal grief of it never transmuted into a poem. Almost mawkish and tritely pompous. But with memorable bits. "Unseen is not unknown. Unkissed is not unloved" and one other parallel line of un– is not un–. With the lines "My soil has cropped its head" which I copied out. He had sent it to Zuk[7], who liked two stanzas, not the other four. But not the ones I liked. He shook his head a little sadly. "I shall have to work on it some more. It should be possible. It should be."

Remarked of the new poem, "It is something I owe myself. That I owe to my past. And there are others." But the effort to bring them to what

---

[5] Tom Pickard (b. 1946). English poet from Newcastle-upon-Tyne, who was instrumental in Bunting returning to writing. Edited *King Ida's Watch Chain* (1965), a single-issue periodical which showcased Bunting's work—see note 11 below. His poetry was also published by Fulcrum Press, Bunting's first London publisher, but most of his available work is now published by Flood Editions of Chicago.

[6] This poem was not collected until after Bunting's death and is included in the *Complete Poems* ed. Richard Caddel (Tarset: Bloodaxe Books 2000; New York: New Directions 2003).

[7] Louis Zukofsky (1904-1978), American poet. He edited *An Objectivist Anthology* in 1932, which included poems by Bunting, alongside Oppen, Reznikoff, Rakosi, Williams and Zukofsky himself, as well as other less obvious contributors, such as Mary Butts and Robert McAlmon.

More Words

he felt they deserved, was almost too much. Next year he would be 65. While there, an anthology arrived from Philadelphia. Co-edited by Ezra Pound. And we both laugh in glee, that he has two poems in it, and only one each for Eliot, William Carlos Williams, Marianne Moore etc. I remark, "But you must be getting a little tired of the 'Morpethshire Farmer'.[8] You'll notice we didn't ask you to read *that* last night." He laughs. "Yes, I can see it's going to be to me what 'The Lake Isle' was to Yeats!"

On the way back down, driving through the fog in Lancashire (freezing up on the radiator) I tell Michael about how he once slept with a Persian whore at the expense of His Majesty's Government, to get information about the Russians. That he was once given ½ a squadron of Spitfires and ½ a squadron of Mosquitos, and a free hand, to clear the Adriatic of German reconnaissance planes. "We did." And Michael tells me of, at the Rutherfords, some talk of sexual morality and he tells of a visit to the head of the Shi'a sect of Islam, in Iraq, on official business. A very saintly man, who has since become so venerated since his death. "He entertained me very well. A full set of courses, and wines, and coffees. And then he asked me, 'Do you prefer girls or boys?' It was only right he should." Apparently, too, he *did* enjoy that hospitality. Another time, in Sicily, he swapped a bottle of Scotch he had got from Malta for two motorbikes, BSAs. His Spitfire mechanics took one, and "did things to it." According to B.—though I found this hard to believe—they put in a pair of Rolls Royce Spitfire cylinders. He clocked 110 mph on it, on the airstrip. Another time, drove it all the way up to the rim of the Mt. Etna crater. And as we drove in the fog, Michael says, in glee, "He's the poet for *us*!"

After the Sunday afternoon reading (Mike & I) at the Morden Tower, we go to the Rutherfords—B., Tom & Connie, Mike & I, with half a dozen others including a couple of people from the university. I have to go to see some personal friends for tea, and they play the entire Creeley tape. After I get back, Basil reads—Tom working the tape recorder. The atmosphere intensely exciting, as if we'd been building up to it all day, and for years. His voice suddenly tremendous, full of energy, so that

---

[8] 'The Complaint of the Morpethshire Farmer', in Bunting's *First Book of Odes*.

it's hard to believe at times, that it comes from this aging man. Singing where appropriate imitating accents & voices flawlessly. There are tears in my eyes. That hypnotised silence. He reads Samangan[9], and the 200 some steps[10], etc. then 'The Well of Lycopolis', saying, "I didn't read it at the Tower reading. I was a bit worried they might turn us out if I did." We are stunned by it. And he says, that when first printed in *Poetry* magazine, he received letters about it from all over the world. But he himself feels doubtful about it. "If I were to write it now, I'd do it differently. I can't help thinking it is flawed." About 'The Orotava Road'—"It's a tribute to Dr Williams. Just a deliberate exercise in his style. Trying to use what he discovered. That's all it is." He is getting a little tired, but shows no sign of it while actually reading. And we persuade him to read the 'Chomei'. A long thing—that he sustains perfectly. A proper finish. The tape giving out, alas, a page before.

It was Basil's idea, the name, *King Ida's Watch Chain*.[11] What the local people call a huge anchor chain dredged up from the sea which hangs in the hall at Bamburgh Castle.

Once he wrote rather a sharp review or comment in *Hound and Horn*, on something by Yvor Winters, who in turn wrote to him in Italy, making a physical challenge of it! It so happened that Gene Tunney[12] was there, and wrote back for him, saying that he (Tunney) would accept the challenge on Bunting's behalf. They didn't hear from Winters again!

He said, "I've done most of the things a man *ought* to do." He repeated this several times. A sense of what may be *known* by a man, directly. But then qualified it, a little sadly, "well most of the things, 75% anyway. But I never learned to fly. It is one of my regrets. And I'm too old now. My eyesight is too bad." (He uses two different pairs of glasses).

---

[9] Untitled poem n° 32 in Bunting's *First Book of Odes*, "Let them remember Samangan, the bridge and tower…"
[10] This refers to the untitled poem n° 26 in the *First Book of Odes*, which begins "Two hundred and seven paces / from the tram-stop / to the door…"
[11] Published in Autumn 1965, and edited by Tom Pickard, this was intended to be a periodical, but only one issue appeared. It contained poems by Bunting, early photos of the poet, essays on his work, reprints of reviews and a facsimile of a manuscript.
[12] Tunney (1897-1978) was World Heavyweight Boxing Champion 1926-28.

When first in Persia, one morning a man arrived at the door with a horse for him. Sent for his personal use by one of the Persian generals. Bunting had to apologise, that he could not ride. Then the message came back, "We will teach you!" He attended the cavalry riding school, run by the acknowledged best cavalry teacher in the world. "The first day we started off bareback, riding facing backwards. The next day we were standing up on the horse. It went on like that. By the end of the week, we were getting off and on the horse as it galloped. To finish, we all rode to the top of a steep mountain, and back again. Coming down the horses were sliding most of the way on their rumps. But I learned to ride!"

Just before we left he remarked on the pleasures left to him. "I can still read. I read Dante, Homer, Firdosi. That's all, really, now. I still read them."

He saw two public hangings. One was of a doctor, who had murdered a lot of patients, for money. But he was away off at the edge of the crowd, and there really to keep an eye out for undercover agents. The other was a rebel who had been a ringleader in a conspiracy. He had helped to uncover the plot, and had to attend as the official British representative. "They did it from one of the city gates. Just drove a lorry underneath. He choked to death. It isn't very pleasant at all."

About war, "It's all very different. There's a tremendous excitement. An exhilaration. So that you aren't really allowed to get frightened. And it usually all happens so quickly."

He had been intelligence officer for a fighter squadron in the Mediterranean area. In the Sicily invasion, he and two others were working at the operations HQ, and had direct contact with Eisenhower. But they lost very few pilots at all. They were highly skilled. When Normandy came up, the squadron was taken back to England to do cover work and close support, because of this. "It was terrible. Even during the Battle of Britain, if a pilot did two or three sorties in a day, it was considered a lot. My pilots were going out six or seven times in a day. Working low all the time. They were just worn out completely, in no time. We lost nearly every one. Mostly just fatigue. There is one left. He's still living in England. I hear from him sometimes. After that, they wanted to put me on with some safe squadron, just doing patrol work in the north sea. It would have been easy. But I didn't want that, then." That was when he managed to get out to Persia instead.

He said to me, "If I have anything to say to you young people, it's that you tend to think in very short lines, in bits. I think your sense of the longer rhythmic structure is defective." And he spoke, cautiously, of the sense of rhythmical structure, which can run through an entire page. I showed him my 'Sierra' poem and the running phrases, and he read it for me. I was astonished. I had myself failed to read it aloud, as I had intended it. He also remarked, "They are very near to Alexandrines"—and that "I don't think you even need to break the lines up as you have..." I said that I wanted to send him my 'Gilgamesh', for his comments, and suggestions, but he said "I'm not much good at that. Now Zukofsky could give you more help. But I think you really need someone of your own generation for that, not me." Of the musical, the verbal sound quality of his poetry he said "It's onomatopoeia. That's all it is. It's actually very simple".

Of the remarks attributed to him by Dallam Flynn[13] in the famous, or infamous, preface, he seemed quite surprised. I think, myself, that what happened is that Flynn made some Poundian & more emphatic translation of remarks by Bunting in a letter. It's the tone that is wrong.

I asked him if he could think of any other British poets of his (or near) generation, who had been unjustly neglected or forgotten. "There isn't anyone else. The only one whom I think had something of the genuine article in him, is Dylan Thomas." I asked about Joseph Gordon Macleod[14]. He laughed. "In 1932, we were asked to pick who we

---

[13] Dallam Flynn, publisher of Bunting's *Poems 1950* at The Cleaner's Press, Galveston, TX. Flynn wrote the preface, which was somewhat disparaging of contemporary British poetry, and of Eliot. It was suggested in later years that this had persuaded Eliot not to take the book on at Faber, although this seems speculative. Bunting had not seen the preface, or indeed any proofs, before the book's publication.

[14] Joseph Gordon Macleod (1903-1984). One of the "lost" British modernist poets, he was rated highly by both Pound and Bunting in the '30s. His most notable work is

thought would come to something. Ezra picked Macleod and I picked Auden."

After *RM*[15] had been published he exchanged a few letters with Auden, who asked him to a meeting at a pub near Fleet Street. "Day Lewis was there, and others of the gang. They were just getting known. I found them dreadfully boring. Then another young man came in, whom I liked. We went off together, and had a grand time. He was Welsh. I liked him. It was Thomas. But I never saw any of them again."

He felt that the 'Four Quartets' were badly flawed. And that Eliot has a dead ear. "He beats a drum. His beat is too obvious and boring. It goes thump thump thump. It isn't even as subtle as Kipling can be. Kipling can be very good, you know". He also admired Hardy. "That's one of my regrets. That I never went to see the old man. It would have been quite easy. But I never went."

I spoke of the lack of overall structure in the *The Cantos*, in *Paterson*, in Zukofsky's '*A*' etc. and he remarked, "Dante spent many years just *planning* his poem, before he even began to write it. He wasn't in a hurry. I think, too, of your generation, you all write too much. Though I must admit that most important writers have always written a lot."

---

perhaps the long poem *The Ecliptic* (London: Faber & Faber 1930). The only modern edition of his poetry is *Cyclic Serial Zeniths from the Flux. Selected Poems* ed. Andrew Duncan (Brighton: Waterloo Press 2009).
[15] *Redimiculum Matellarum* (Milan 1930), Bunting's first book.

An Arlespenny

Some notes on the poetry of Basil Bunting

Bunting's poems are difficult to obtain and are as yet largely unpublished in this country. Yet they are read more widely and with more attention than ever. This may be irrelevant as we read them; but is one testimony to their permanence. Few of his generation (he is 65 this year) have had their work survive so well and against such odds.

What is most immediately striking is the continual melodic invention. This is distinct and quite personal in the main bulk of his verse. Although the debt to both Pound and Yeats is explicit in some of the very early pieces, it does not repeat what they have done. What is more remarkable, it does not repeat itself.

> Blind Bashshar bin Burd Saw,
> doubted, glanced back,
> guessed whence, speculated whither.
> Panegyrists, blinder and deaf,
> prophets, exegesists, counsellors of patience,
> lie in wait for blood,
> every man with a net.[1]

> Rinsed in cool sleep day will renew the summer
> lightnings. Leave it to me. Only a savage's
> lusts explode slapbang at the first touch like bombs.[2]

> A fowler spreading his net
> over the barley, calls,
> calls on a rubber reed.
> Grain's nods in reply.
> Poppies blue upon white
> wake to the sun's frown.

---

[1] Basil Bunting 'The Spoils' (1932) *Complete Poems* ed. Richard Caddel (Tarset: Bloodaxe Books 2000; New York: New Directions 2003).
[2] Basil Bunting, poem nº 9 from the *First Book of Odes*, ibid.

More Words

> Scut of gazelle dances and bounces
> out of the afternoon.
> Owl and wolf to the night.[3]

> On a terrace over a pool
> vafur, vodka, tea,
> resonant verse spilled
> from Onsori, Sa'di,
> till the girls' mutter is lost
> in whispers of stream and leaf...[4]

What is immediately noticeable is the resource with which he utilises the simple effects of assonance and alliteration. This is never done for its own sake but to advance a pattern and to provide substance for the rhythmical changes. Where it is obtrusive it is always for some particular emphasis. To use an overworked simile, he orchestrates the meaning. Even when the tone is bitter or sarcastic, his concern is for the ear of the reader, that we should *hear* and not just *read*.

> An arles, an arles for my hiring,
> O master of singers, an arlespenny!
>
> —Well sung singer, said Apollo,
> but in this trade we pay no wages.[5]

> Yes, it's slow, docked of armours,
>   docked of the doubtless efficacious
> bottled makeshift, gin; but who'd risk being bored stiff
> every night listening to father's silly sarcasms?[6]

---

[3] Basil Bunting from 'The Spoils', op.cit.
[4] ibid
[5] Basil Bunting, poem nº 12 from the *First Book of Odes*, ibid.
[6] Basil Bunting, beginning of untitled poem in the Overdrafts section of *Complete Poems*, op. cit.

What mournful stave, what bellow shakes the grove?
O, it is Attis grieving for his testicles!
Attis stiffening amid the snows
and the wind whining through his hair and fingers![7]

In 'The Orotava Road' he makes use of a triplet structure which, while anticipating William Carlos Williams' use of a similar device, is distinctively his own. In fact, without forcing the comparison unduly, Bunting's use may offer a greater variety of pace. (It is characteristic that, having done this one poem thoroughly, he went on to other things.)

>   Milkmaids, friendly girls between
>   fourteen and twenty
>   or younger, bolt upright on small
> trotting donkeys that bray (they arch their
>   tails a few inches
>   from the root, stretch neck and jaw forward
> to make the windpipe a trumpet)
>   chatter. Jolted
>   cans clatter. The girl's smiles repeat
> the black silk curve of the wimple
>   under the chin.
>   Their hats are absurd doll's hats
> or flat-crowned to take a load.
>   All have fine eyes.[8]

The central concern of Bunting in his poems is the slightness of the individual under the span of Time and before Death; and the courage, absurdity, pathos, and sheer variety of means by which men face their destiny. One such means is the making of poems.

The expression of this ranges from his version of 'Villon':

Remember, imbeciles and wits,
Sots and ascetics, fair and foul,
Young girls with little tender tits,
That DEATH is written over all.[9]

---

[7] Basil Bunting, from 'Attis: Or Something Missing', *Complete Poems*. op.cit.
[8] Basil Bunting, from 'The Orotava Road', *Complete Poems*. op.cit.
[9] Basil Bunting, from 'Villon', *Complete Poems*. op.cit.

More Words

Through the good humour of:

> ...As for my heart, that may as well be forgotten
> or labelled: Owner will dispose of same.
> to a good home, refs. exchgd., h. & c.,
> previous experience desired but not essential
> or let on a short lease to suit convenience.[10]

The dignity of his translation from Firdosi (classic Persian poet):

> I ask the just Creator
> so much refuge from Time
> that a tale of mine may remain in the world
> from this famous book of the ancients...[11]

The ignominy of a Renaissance incident:

> ...the Duke thought it opportune
> to put an end to Vitellozo and Liverotto,
> and had them led out to a suitable place and strangled.
> Neither said anything worthy of the occasion...[12]

The destruction of one pursued by the Furies:

> He will shrink, his manhood leave him, slough self-aware
> the last skin of the flayed: despair.
> He will nurse his terror carefully, uncertain
> even of death's solace...[13]

The ravages of age:

> "Blotched belly, slack buttock and breast,
> there's little to strip for now.
> A few years makes a lot of difference.

---

[10] Basil Bunting, 'Personal Column', from *First Book of Odes*, *Complete Poems*. op.cit.
[11] Basil Bunting, untitled poem, "When the sword of sixty comes nigh his head", from the Overdrafts section of *Complete Poems*. op.cit.
[12] Basil Bunting, 'How Duke Valentine Contrived', from the Overdrafts section of *Complete Poems*. op.cit.
[13] Basil Bunting, 'Chorus of Furies', from the *First Book of Odes* in *Complete Poems*. op.cit.

> Would you have known me?
> Poor old fools,
> gabbing about our young days..."[14]

to the far perspectives of 'The Spoils'. This is a long poem that was first printed in *Poetry* in 1951, and more recently broadcast on the BBC. The first section deals with aspects of the Semitic mind and experience, both Arab and Jew, essentially Mesopotamia, both past and present.

> Thirty gorged vultures on an ass's carcase
> jostle, stumble, flop aside, drunk with flesh,
> too heavy to fly, wings deep with inner gloss.
> Lean watches, then debauch:
> after long alert, stupidity...
>
> [...]
>
> When Tigris floods, snakes swarm in the city,
> coral, jade, jet, between jet and jade, yellow,
> enamelled toys. Toads
> crouch on doorsteps. Jerboas
> weary, unwary, may be taught to feed
> from a fingertip. Dead camels, dead Kurds,
> unmanageable rafts of logs
> hinder the ferryman...
>
> [...]
>
> Bound to beasts' udders, rags no dishonour,
> not by much intercourse ennobled,
> multitude of books, bought deference:
> meagre flesh tingling to a mouthful of water,
> apt to no servitude, commerce or special dexterity,
> at night after prayers recite the sacred
> enscrolled poems...
>
> [...]

---

[14] Basil Bunting, 'The Well of Lycopolis', *Complete Poems*. op.cit.

More Words

> What's begotten on a journey but souvenirs?
> Life we give and take, pence in a market,
> without noting beggar, dealer, changer;
> pence we drop in the sawdust with spilt wine.[15]

The central section is concerned with aspects of the Persian civilisation. In the last section the attention shifts to scenes of the Second World War in North Africa and the Mediterranean; and finally comes home to the north.

> Flight-lieutenant Idema, half course run
> that started from Grand Rapids, Michigan,
> wouldn't fight for Roosevelt,
> 'that bastard Roosevelt', pale
> at Malta's ruins, enduring
> a jeep guarded like a tyrant.
> In British uniform and pay
> for fun of fighting and pride,
> for Churchill on foot alone,
> clowning with a cigar was lost
> in best blues and his third plane that day.
>
> Broken booty but usable
> along the littoral, frittering into the south.
> We marvelled, careful of carters and minefields,
> noting a new-painted recognisance
> on a fragment of fuselage, sand drifting into dumps,
> a tank's turret twisted skyward…
>
> […]
> From Largo Law look down,
> moon and dry weather, look down
> on convoy marshalled, filing between mines.
> Cold northern clear sea-gardens
> between Lofoten and Spitzbergen,
> as good a grave as any earth or water.
> What else do we live for and take part,
> we who would share the spoils?[16]

---

[15] Basil Bunting from 'The Spoils', op.cit.
[16] ibid

An Arlespenny

For myself, I re-read Bunting's poems for many pleasures, but chiefly these: the conviction of direct knowledge of physical experience, and: an unfailing devotion to the poem as a construction of words to be both said and heard, and not merely read with the eye. Bunting's poems ask us to experience them much as one might any other bodily sensation. Certainly they ask to be fondled with the tongue, to feel the roughness of the consonants, taste the flavour of the vowels. There are times when I come close to smelling them:

> ...I remember during the War
> kids carrying the clap to school under their pinnies,
> studying Belgian atrocities in the Sunday papers
> or the men pissing in the backstreets; and grown women
> sweating their shifts sticky at the smell of khaki,
> every little while.
> Love's an encumbrance to them who
> rinse carefully before using...[17]

There is the surprise of the observed detail, as in this description of an earthquake:

> A child building a mud house against a wall:
> I saw him crushed suddenly, his eyes hung
> from their orbits like two tassels.[18]

Even the humour is actual, every step and moment to the full:

> Two hundred and seven paces
>   from the tram-stop
> to the door,
>
> a hundred and forty-six thousand
>   four hundred
> seconds ago,
>
> two hundred and ninety-six thousand
>   eight hundred
> kisses or thereabouts; what else

---

[17] Basil Bunting, 'The Well of Lycopolis', *Complete Poems*. op.cit.
[18] Basil Bunting, 'Chomei at Toyama', *Complete Poems*. op.cit.

More Words

    let him say who saw and let
        him who is able
  do like it…[19]

Then there is the practical man who knows the necessities of poverty:

    The Lady asked the Poet:
    Why do you wear your raincoat in the drawing-room?
    He answered: Not to show
    my arse sticking out of my trousers.[20]

But it is by the voice that I am held. Not sound in any way cultivated for itself, as separate; but spoken and heard with the full sense that it is only by articulate speech that we can know anything, and that no word exists until it is spoken and heard. It is the achievement of Bunting's poetry that we hear and apprehend with no sense of any separation:

    Have you seen a falcon stoop
    accurate, unforeseen
    and absolute, between
    windripples over harvest? Dread
    of what's to be, is and has been—
    were we not better dead?
    His wings churn air
    to flight.
    Feathers alight
    with sun, he rises where
    dazzle rebuts our stare,
    wonder our flight.[21]

---

[19] Basil Bunting, untitled poem "Two hundred and seven paces…" from *First Book of Odes, Complete Poems.* op.cit.
[20] Basil Bunting, untitled poem "An arles, an arles for my hiring…" from *First Book of Odes*, op.cit.
[21] Basil Bunting from 'The Spoils', op.cit.

The Poet as Makar

The poet as makar. Not as sage or seer, or recorder of the human condition, or shaper of texts suitable for the educational system, or cultural analyst, or lover, or popular entertainer, or even as spy. These, and many other activities, are all valid but peripheral.

The poet as someone who makes or composes poems. Poems as constructions, as patterns of words which when heard (or in our culture, predominantly read but nevertheless finally "heard" in what might be called the inner ear) give us that experience of something we label as poetry. And which other sorts of verbal expression do not.

Common observation confirms that what one hearer registers as poetry is not always what another may recognize. Conventions and assumptions in regard to this also vary from generation to generation and are much shaped by cultural assumptions. As indeed by linguistic patterns. Expressions of religious instruction, of cultural admonition, of factual or fictional narrative, or of personal relationships can occur in any use of language, and do frequently (and often particularly powerfully) in poems, but in themselves do not make such sequences of words poems.

Much has been written about Basil's poems in the past thirty or so years. But this sense of *makar* was one principal quality of his work that first attracted and struck me in the later 1950s. What I wrote at about that time expressed it as:

> ...marking fit words together,
> meshed and wedged in time,
> to survive by artefact...[1]

Or:

> What is most immediately striking is the continual melodic invention... more remarkably, it does not repeat itself... [with] an unfailing devotion to the poem as a construction of words to be both said and heard...[2]

---

[1] Gael Turnbull, 'A Fanfare', *King Ida's Watch Chain* (periodical), ed. Tom Pickard. Newcastle upon Tyne, 1965.
[2] Gael Turnbull, 'An Arlespenny', *ibid*. See also pp53-60 of this volume.

Having written a poem which did certain things, there was no point in composing another to the same pattern. This is a counsel of perfection that no one can totally realize. We can recognize familiar devices throughout the bulk of his work, and indeed can take pleasure in this. But the push to not merely echo but contrive afresh is always there.

I don't agree with those who regret that he did not produce another work directly comparable to 'Briggflatts'. A poem such as 'Stones trip Coquet burn' does not easily lend itself to volumes of literary comment but is no less—perhaps even more?—valid as an extraordinary production. Like any poet or writer commenting on their own intentions and practice, what he said (and wrote) needs to be considered with interest but no undue reverence. His emphasis on "the sound it makes" was a necessary one but words are not abstract tones, they are vehicles for expression and meaning and his own work is rich and subtle in that. He scorned blether and nonsense, however mellifluous.

I must admit to being disconcerted by the posthumously published *A Note on Briggflatts*.[3] True, he begins, and ends, with the apology that it is necessary corrective, even defence against misrepresentation. But all that verbiage about the various philosophers and "the pulse of God's blood in our veins"? Perhaps he had begun to absorb something of what he protests against? The younger man would, I believe, have scorned such preoccupations, interesting as they can be, and valid in their own context. There are also the bawdy poems which (for reasons best known to the publishers and editor) have been excluded even from the Uncollected Poems. This is as valid an area for poetry as any other, if more limited, and of those of which I know (there are probably others) as inventive and incisive as any in the official canon. If they are also fun, he is not afraid to celebrate that elsewhere. Dunbar, as an exemplar of all that a makar might be, would—I am confident—have acclaimed and enjoyed them. As would have Burns.

---

[3] Basil Bunting, *A Note on Briggflatts* (Durham: Basil Bunting Poetry Archive, Durham University 1989)

The Spoils, a long poem by Basil Bunting[1]
Migrant Press, 7 Endwood Court Road, Birmingham 20. 5/-

A pivotal work in the over-all pattern of Bunting's poetry. Written and first published in 1951. The complexity of the verse (use of alliteration, assonance, rhyme and rhythmical variation) more resourceful than in the various Sonatas (1920s and '30s) but not yet as fully developed as in the much longer 'Briggflatts' (1965)

The Spoils are the spoils of war. In this case, the war of 1939–1945. What Bunting, personally, "got out of the war". Which sent him to the Middle East. The record of what one man was able to salvage from one period of his life.

In three sections. The first: the sons of Shem, the semitic mind and expression, both Arab and Jew, through the voices of various personae. Second: Persia, which is part of the experience of the first section but crystallised out from it. A few indicators of the background and history of Persian culture. Then concentrating on everyday knowledge of it. Ending upon a single image of a falcon diving over a harvest field. Third: starting near to where, geographically, the previous section ended, it narrows down even more specifically upon the details of personal happenings in the war, moving away from Persia through the Mediterranean. At the end "coming home" to the "North".

The movement of the whole composition is from the past to the present, (and at the end, looking forward into the future towards death) from the archetypical to the personal, from the thronged variegation of the Middle East to a final glimpse of a cold flat northern sea.

As background to the intense realization of physical experience, there is an awareness of death. Struck in the first lines of the poem:

> Man's life so little worth
> do we fear to take or lose it?

Of which war is one aspect. To be entered upon for what it may reveal. As an accentuation of all experience. Picked up again at the end of the first and second sections, and in the very last lines of the poem:

---

[1] Quotations from Basil Bunting, 'The Spoils', are reprinted from the *Complete Poems*, edited by Richard Caddel (Tarset: Bloodaxe Books 2000; New York: New Directions 2003).

> ...as good a grave as any, earth or water.
> What else do we live for and take part,
> we who would share the spoils?

Which links with the title through the epigraph which is from the Koran: "The spoils are for God" or "belong to God". However much we may experience, whatever loot we may bring home, it is never wholly or merely ours.

Bunting, Brigflatts and Margaret Greenbank

Gael Turnbull was very touched by the reunion, which he helped bring about, of Basil Bunting and Margaret Greenbank—Basil's lost love Peggy, focus of his most famous poem, 'Briggflatts'.

Basil scorned biography, especially autobiography, for the good reason that it was the poems that mattered, not the personal life or circumstances of whoever composed them. Also that it encouraged self deception and conceit. This did not prevent him from being one of the most interesting and amusing story tellers of events from his own experience, and he took evident relish and satisfaction in the telling, as he does in various interviews.

There is also respect for honesty, for "what really happened", difficult as that can be.

I always recall him saying, "I have done most of the things a man ought to do". His one regret was that he was never able to learn to fly an aeroplane, for which he blamed his poor eyesight.

Most of his anecdotes have been recorded by others. What I narrate here has the excuse, if such is needed, that I had a particular role in the episode. There is also the fact that it is relevant to the composition of his most admired poem. It is also of intrinsic human interest, and Hardy might have written parts.

In fact, he was not unaware of this, remarking in one letter (21 June 1965) on the history of Peggy's family "…like a series of stories by Hardy, all sad, some tragic. And what am I doing in the most melodramatic novel of them all?"

In early April 1965, I arranged some readings for him in the Midlands, including one at Nottingham and significantly at Leicester where G.S. Fraser was teaching (one of the very first to recognise his achievement when *Poems 1950* had been published) as well as local private occasions. He wished to visit London (chiefly to see D.G. Bridson, I think) and I had the happy inspiration to arrange for him to stay with Stuart Montgomery in their flat at Belsize Park Gardens. Stuart had written to me shortly before, ordering some Migrant Press items and a community of interest was quickly recognised. Much came of that visit, and by later

More Words

in the summer *Loquitur*[1] was in active preparation.

By 27 March, a draft of the first four parts (and opening of the fifth) of 'Briggflatts' had been completed and indeed carbon copies of this were used to try to publicise the April readings, and I wrote and circulated a brief appreciation of his poems up to that date, later incorporated in *King Ida's Watch Chain*.[2]

In early May, with Jonnie & the children, we made a visit to Shadingfield. Although nearly finished, he was still working on the poem.

On 10 May he wrote "...sad to find the house so empty since your battalions left".

I was already aware of many of the circumstances of his attachment to Brigflatts, the place. We had been planning to travel back to Malvern & Cradley by the quickest and easiest route but he became insistent that we ought to go by way of Sedbergh. I was not averse to the more scenic journey but the children would find the longer travel difficult, as the driving would be.

However, I could sense that it was important for him, and I didn't take too much persuading. I knew that without a car, it was difficult for him to visit himself and I was aware of the relationship of the place to the poem, and felt a sense of pilgrimage, even curiosity.

When we stopped with the VW mini-bus in the lay-by at the top of the lane, I even had my photograph taken beside the little signpost. Jonnie had no great wish to explore and the children were tired, so they waited in the bus. Perhaps I also wished to be alone to relish the occasion.

I had only vague ideas as to what I might find down the lane, and it all seemed quite shut in, and very silent except for the murmur of the river. I went into the Meeting House, looked around, and sat for a while.

Years ago, I had attended a *meeting*, and knew something of the Friends and the significance of the place and the silence. Eventually,

---

[1] Basil Bunting *Loquitur* (London: Fulcrum Press 1965). This volume was, in effect a second, and slightly expanded, edition of *Poems 1950*; one poem was removed, three added, a couplet was inserted in the *Odes*, and the positioning of 'The Orotava Road' changed. Fulcrum Press had already published an edition of the *First Book of Odes*, and were to follow *Loquitur* with *Briggflatts* and then a full *Collected Poems*.

[2] One-off issue of a magazine, dedicated entirely to Bunting's work, and edited by Tom Pickard.

(perhaps as I got up to leave) an older man appeared from the attached flat. He showed interest in why I had come, and from where.

There were regular visitors from all over the world. I explained my distant association with and interest in the movement, then added that I had a friend who had known the place as a boy, in fact had spent school holidays there and that I thought there had been a mason's yard nearby.

He looked very doubtful about this, may have even said that he thought I was mistaken. Luckily I persisted, and mentioned that I had been told that there was a stonemason who had lived there.

He reconsidered, saying something to the effect, "Come to think of it, there used to be some bits of marble in the farmyard at the end. But that would be a very long time ago. A stonemason? Yes, I think there was. Long before my time."

He then added something about "I think it's his daughter who still lives in the house across the lane. She's very friendly. She'd know more about it. Why don't you have a word with her? She enjoys talking about old times."

I felt a lurch of panic. The mason's daughter? Was I going to knock on that door?

As I walked back up the lane, I was full of troubled thoughts. Had I any business blundering into someone else's past? We drove home.

At first I wondered if it might be best to say nothing to Basil. I could have imagined more than was potentially there, or it was all a misunderstanding. Yet it was too much of a coincidence to be dismissed. And what if that *was* Peggy in the house across the lane?

I decided that the best thing to do was to write an account of my visit as accurately and fully as I could and send to Basil, without speculation. Let him make of it what he wished. I had done all I could. And had he not, in a sense, sent me on his own behalf?

But my speculation, even if not explicit, must have come through my narrative.

He wrote back almost immediately, on the 13 May. "You knew of course that your report on Briggflatts [his spelling] would strike very deep. Yet what you tell me is no more than I foresaw and expected before I began to write the poem… But first I must be sure… Her elder sister had no health. Still, unexpected things happen, the weakling often survives... It would be cruel to leave her to hear of the poem from anyone else. And if she is quite indifferent, it would even be discourteous."

But another remark in the letter reveals how deeply shaken he was, and he notes "She has been with me all this half century often when nobody else was."

Three days later, on 16 May he wrote "...I finished [the poem] last night towards midnight... Finding the distance of certain stars solved the last problem of construction."

A little later, probably in reply to something I wrote, on the 26th, he wrote "Yes, of course, I did send you to Brigflatts, expecting that you would find something very much like you did find: hoping so, yet never having really faced the matter..."

From a remark in a letter of 17 June it is clear that he still thought it was "Peggy" in the house across from the Meeting House.

Basil did not have a car. Edmond, a cousin of Sima [Basil's wife], who stayed with them, did have, but Basil felt unable, even unwilling, to ask him to go (though he did later).

On the weekend of 18-20 June 1965, he went himself. The account is caustic about the reliability and extent of public transport, and he needed to take a taxi from Penrith. On Monday (21st) he wrote me a long letter, obviously finding relief from the emotional tension by pouring it out. He had no one else to confide in:

"Such a weekend. My mind and emotions in a turmoil. No, it was not Peggy, but her sister Cissie. Peggy is alive and married, elsewhere..." He discovered that she lived with her husband, Edward Edwards, at Hope in Shropshire, had had three children (two tragically dead when young, with one, Gillian, in America), taught in the village school. Her husband worked in the Birmingham area (Wolverhampton, as I recall) in the car industry, away for 3-4 days at a time in lodgings, then home again.

The letter ends with a handwritten postscript "Changed, all changed. A different world."

However, no immediate effort was made to inform or contact Peggy.

Then, in July, Peggy and Edward visited Cissie at Brigflatts as they often did. Her attachment to the place had remained constant, and it had been their family home. While there, Cissie found the occasion to tell Peggy, and show her the poem to read while Edward happened to be out of the house.

The exact sequence after that is obscure to me. Did he write first, or did she? It is not that relevant. On 22 July Basil mentioned in a letter "She has written—such a letter."

His first to her was guarded, knowing that her husband would read it. But he was able to time further letters so that they arrived during the days that Edward was away. At some point that summer, Peggy wrote to her daughter Gillian (who was, as I recall, in Colorado) who also wrote to Basil, who himself made another visit to Cissie at Brigflatts at the end of July.

The coincidence that Hope, on the Bishop's Castle/Shrewsbury road, not far from the Welsh border, was less than a couple of hours from where I lived at Bridge House, has further resonances with Hardy perhaps. It certainly struck me quite forcibly. If I had not actually driven past her house, I already knew the area well, and it facilitated a visit.

Basil made covert arrangements with Peggy and came down to us by train late in October, when he had some leave from his work at the newspaper in Newcastle. But first, that weekend, I took him in the car down to Sherborne in Dorset to see Dorothy Pound.

She was an old and good friend from the days at Rapallo, and Basil often spoke of her kindness and generosity to him then, and his regard for her. She was on a visit from Italy to stay with Omar, Elizabeth and the grandchildren.

It was a memorable occasion for me also, and I was presented to Dorothy. I felt somewhat as if I were being allowed to glimpse a holy relic, or were visiting royalty, or had been granted a private view of a rare collector's item (from Edwardian London) in the V & A.

She always kept something of this quality for me, though was warm and generous in her personal manner, despite being enshrined in the patterns of her origin from which she could not escape. There was also a sense (very real) that for her the everyday practicalities were irrelevant, and best done by servants. Elizabeth maintained that she was incapable of making even a cup of tea for herself, living for books, art, higher things, the only worthwhile priorities… and why not, if she could?

Peggy did ring us, by arrangement, for final confirmation. It was thus that on Tuesday (or Wednesday) the 26th (or 27th) that I first drove Basil, in my little Fiat 500, up to Hope. He had bought, the day before in Worcester, the collected poems of Yeats as a present. It cost 25/-, which he did not have but borrowed from me, insisting on writing me a cheque for the amount. I still have that cheque, uncashed.

We had directions, of course. The house was on the right, facing on to the road and quite close, with the main garden extending northwards from it. I left Basil at the door and drove off. I can't recall if I even waited to see if anyone came to the door to let him in.

It was obviously best for them to make the encounter without me, and I went for a walk for a few hours on the nearby hills. I think my ordinance survey showed remains of a stone circle somewhere but it was a strange sensation, wondering what was happening, after such a long time. Peggy remarked later of my "walking on Stapely Hill to give us some little time alone."

By arrangement I came back about 4.30 or so, for tea, and we drove back to Bridge House as it was getting dark. Impossible to describe them together. The intensity of their emotion and happiness was not uncomfortable, if amazing. My own apprehensions soon eased. Even their parting did not seem strained or painful. After all, they had known each other for a very long time, whatever the gap of years between.

There was no immediate repeat visit to Hope, though there were visits again by Peggy and Edward to Brigflatts, and also by Basil. Soon Cissie came back to visit Wylam, thanks to Edmond's car. Eventually, Basil was introduced to Edward, but only as an old and good friend of the family. Basil, to his surprise, found him personally unobjectionable. This masquerade succeeded for a time.

I don't know at what point Edward read the poem, if he ever did in detail, or what significance he gave to the opening section, but anyway it was obviously all a very long time ago.

But revelation came. Basil told me, and with evident relish, that the persistence and intensity of Peggy's attachment to him, and his to her, eventually became evident to Edward. I think it was on a visit to Wylam that Edward is said to have suddenly awoken Peggy in the middle of the night, unable to sleep or contain it any longer: "You are in love with Basil!" or words to that effect.

But prior to this, as afterwards, they corresponded surreptitiously, and at the end of 1965 or in Jan 1966, Basil had sent her an extended and detailed account of his life since their parting, a confession of some sort, which he may have told her to destroy after she had had time to absorb it. On 6 Feb 1966, he wrote of her "…still getting my infamous life-story by heart … and will take a little time to digest … I want her attached to the living man, warts and all."

He was anxious for her, and about her health, and I even went up to Hope to see her on his behalf on one occasion, and was able to reassure. On 18 Jan 66 he had written "I don't know how I could go on if she were taken from me…"

He had of course by then spent very little time with her, even less with just the two of them alone. Eventually after a couple of months of planning, he was able to go to Hope again (via Bridge House and my taxi service) to stay for a few days, unknown to Edward who was away working his usual weekly stint.

Thus the practicalities were difficult, as well as the emotional ones. On 3 Sept 66 he wrote "I am suffering from Peggy's determination to have a good conscience… Let people love and unlove without having to go after divorces… I never felt like claiming exclusive rights in any of my women, after I was about 22 or 3, and I don't see why they should require exclusive rights in me. Contracting to keep a household together is a different matter… I was 'faithful' to Marian… but it certainly isn't Marian who loves me in consequence…"

I have no doubt in my mind that he did have hopes that they could make some sort of life together but he had no adequate or secure income (there had been the episode earlier when his circle of friends had to have a "whip around" to bail out the problems of his mortgage on Shadingfield), especially since he had finally left the *Chronicle* (he was over 66).

He was briefly at Buffalo that summer, then Kenner arranged for him to teach at Santa Barbara. He wrote on 9 Sept '66 "Peggy very distressed by my going [to Santa Barbara]… I wish she would come with me…"

Because of unpredictable postal deliveries from America, writing to her at Hope was difficult, as they could not be sure of them arriving while Edward was away. Thus I became the postal go-between. Peggy sent me a bundle of envelopes addressed to herself in her own hand (but with a variety of orthography, in case Edward was unexpectedly at home).

Basil's letters for her would arrive at Bridge House. I would wait until I knew Edward would be away before posting them on in the envelopes she had provided. So far as I know, the local service was sufficiently reliable that there was no mishap. On 3 Dec '66, Basil wrote to me from Santa Barbara "Thank you, postman, on behalf of Peggy" and then on the 24th, "No letters for Peggy until after holidays for obvious reasons" [i.e. Edward was at home over Christmas & New Year].

Sima, of course, was eventually aware of it and mostly scornful, at least affecting not to stoop to jealousy, just remarking "Silly old man!" She was more irate over the money aspects, rightly aware that Basil did not stint himself over his Navy Full Cut or beer at the pub, and complaining that he had no realistic idea of the real costs of running a household.

He seemed more of a grandfather figure in the house, than husband or father. There was also Edmond, who squired Sima about, was involved with her buying and renovating and selling cottages, although also refurbishing Shadingfield. They were sometimes away on holiday together.

After Basil had moved out, Edmond eventually went back to Persia. Basil complained about him not paying his way, even demanding money for reasons that Basil considered spurious. I thought that the ménage often depended on him, especially for keeping the house in good condition.

Tom was still a schoolboy, mostly keeping to himself. Maria was at Art school and had her John, who virtually lived there although his actual home was only a few minutes away. And there always seemed to be some visitor from Persia, sometimes family connections, sometimes friends of friends, plus assorted poets, even academics. The house accommodated us all without obvious indigestion.

I don't have the heart to hunt through subsequent letters to possibly identify the date when they finally parted for the second time. How much was it a mutual decision, how much hers, how much Basil's? I don't know. [Aldritt quotes from a letter to Denis Goacher, that it was Peggy who insisted on the break.] Certainly, as late as 1974, he was still corresponding with her, but unable to go to visit her.

Some of the initial emotional intensity undoubtedly faded. Basil was aware that he had, perhaps once again, upset her life. Peggy was uneasy about it almost from the start.

Whatever the details, a decision was made. Certainly, Peggy could not face abandoning Edward, who had been very upset at the possibility, of which he was aware, even if the practicalities of money would have allowed it.

When Edward eventually died, there was no effort to re-establish contact of which I know. It is possible that I am mistaken, but Basil was not someone, if he had made a decision, to retract. If there was such a move, it was soon abandoned. I lost touch with her after about the end of 1974. When Basil died, I was very conscious of her at the funeral, which was at Brigflatts, much dominated by one of the American daughters from his first marriage. The house, where Cissie had lived, had been sold to strangers.

I was upset by the lack of any mention of her on the occasion, by anyone. Perhaps my own fault.

I did write her a note afterwards, saying how I felt for her, assuming that the news had reached her, and to assure her that she had not been totally forgotten. The letter was returned "No Longer at this Address".

Michael Shayer tracked her down and called on her later, by then in a social services home in Bishop's Castle, where she died.

I feel much regret, indeed shame, that I made so little effort to keep in touch in the later years of her life. So far as I know, her only surviving child, a daughter (Gillian), was still in America.

When I rang the nursing home in the early 1990s to enquire, hoping for a contact address for Gillian, I was told that they no longer had any records about her.

One of the poets who was at Basil's funeral did publish a little account of that event, which, among other stupidities, does contain a reference to her, but derisory in context. I found, and still find it, impossible to forgive, whatever occasioned the remark. She deserved better. Ignorance may be excusable, gratuitous insult is not.

She was a warm and gallant lady, much torn and jolted by the hazards of life and passion. I still have the open ceramic bowl she made and gave me (probably in that winter of 1965/66), with bluish grey slip and a cream glaze, and a simple but elegantly inscribed leaf pattern around the inside of the rim. It is inscribed on the back, into the clay: ME (Margaret Edwards).

October 1999

Basil Bunting with Peggy. Photo by Jonathan Williams.
Reproduced by permission of the Estate of Jonathan Williams.

American and Canadian Poets

A Visit to William Carlos Williams, September, 1958
From the Diary of Gael Turnbull

Sunday I phoned Rutherford. The silliness of it, to make sure that I had him and not his son. Then my name. Instantly he knew it. A childish excitement. "Well, now... well, now... if that doesn't... so where are... My, my!" And so, settled that we were to go the next afternoon.

The chaos of cars, noises, down the canyons between the skyscrapers, to roar through the Lincoln Tunnel under the river (like a packet in a vacuum tube). Out on a maze of overpasses and expressways, dodging the big cars. Out, out, in a landscape of factories and desolate wastes, where a man seemed an impertinence.

Then a sign: Rutherford, and abruptly we were in a small town, trees, grassy lawns, white frame houses, quiet main street, parking meters, tucked away, gentle. (And yet, only a few moments ago, looking back in the rear mirror I had seen the whole skyline of New York, terrible, in the sun, military, metallic, Cyclopean.)

To find Ridge Road. And number nine, it is almost on the main street, practically at the town centre. Workmen hammering, boards lying about. A woman coming out (patient? or son's wife?) to direct us in over the sawdust. Bill (the son) having an afternoon surgery, camped out in the dining room because of the construction. A few women with children. Paintings on the wall, Ben Shahn one.

Then WCW down the stairs. Shorter than I'd thought, and more stocky. Thinning white hair and prominent nose. Fussy and happy. Reached out with both hands to take Jonnie's and mine at once. "So you are here... I can't believe... This is wonderful..."

Then into the drawing room, I talking a bit nervously. To sit... "Just sit for a minute and *look* at each other." And so we looked, all of us grinning, and his eyes twinkling. Moving a little restlessly, but no sign of any paralysis. Kind face, an old man, showing a certain sinking of the flesh, a sort of withdrawal.

And then after he had surveyed us to his satisfaction, we went around the room looking at the paintings. By his brother Ed... and his own mother.

Then Floss came, thinner than WCW, and somehow looking physically stronger. She gives a sense that he, and poetry, and the whole world, are a queer sort of show that she never really had anticipated;

but once it had all happened, she'd go along with it and take part and enjoy it, and observe with a certain wry humour, a kind of reserve, but not aloof really.

So we went upstairs to his study, and we talked the usual things, about our trip over, and being in New York, etc. etc. Sometimes he'd say things that it was hard to quite catch, half-finished phrases, and a nervous speed of voice. It was as if he had opened his mind to you completely, every disconnected fragment that came into his mind.

Then he brings a copy of *Paterson Five,* all ready and inscribed for me, and he says he hopes I'll find something interesting in it (and the humility, that he really isn't very confident, and to think that I would like something in it would be a great pleasure to him). Then I feel desperate that he should do so and give him a drawing of mine, the one of the heraldic beast, the Lion of St. Mark (and this because it is my *own* favourite, and so, in giving it, I feel the greatest loss myself, and hence the greatest satisfaction in the act). And he is duly impressed by its ferocity.

He has just written a poem—*The Nation* asked for one—so he shows it to me, "Now, what do you think of it? I don't know."

The poem is called 'Advice to Mr. Eliot' and it is just that. He urges me, truly concerned, "Now, what *do* you think of it?" Nervously, wanting my approval—yes, I wasn't indulging my fancy, I know that, he wanted my opinion and my approval, or anyone's. And under his eyes, the sudden desperate intent, I can do nothing but say what is in my mind, I can't escape the commitment, "I don't like the last two lines. I'd like it better if you stopped here." Pointing at the sheet. And he looks too, and nods, and nods again, "Yes, yes, so you do think so? Well, maybe you're right. Maybe. I don't know. I'll have to see about it. I wonder. You are probably right. But I don't know."... And he looks a little crestfallen, but only the slightest bit, while I squirm inwardly, trapped by his sincerity.

Then I mention having heard of the work room he used to have and he takes me up to the attic, a bit awkward on the stairs, a typical old attic, but large. "We used to have parties here. Oh, those were wild days! In the twenties and thirties. People would come out here. Drink and girls. We'd goose them from behind as we came up the stairs." And he'd grin, like an impudent urchin…

And all the old magazines and books, and bits of unfinished manuscripts, and all that is left of his writing boards are two or three rickety bits. "I used to have a stove up here, and a telephone, so I could come up and stay here as long as I wanted. I had to get away."

"But it's all gone now. Let's go back to the study. They can get rid of all this junk once I'm dead." Then he talks of Rutherford... No bars. And medicine. "I never had any contact with anyone here. I couldn't live their life. I used to hate it. A poet shouldn't have to live!"—savagely without more explanation and as if it were perfectly obvious...

And then later, "I don't know what it is. It was as if there was a devil in me. I think I believe in the devil. Something in me, that kept at me, wouldn't let me alone, wouldn't let me rest." And then, again, about women, "Oh, Floss, what she's put up with. I don't know how. I was pretty raw in those days. Some of the women, too. It was all wrong. But there it is. I wonder what she thinks of me."

And then, "But we're old now. We're just in the way. The sooner we're gone, the better. We should let Bill take over the house." And then, "I've always felt so lost here, this town, I wanted to get out, I couldn't stick it, so I had to write, you see, there wasn't anything else I suppose. And now my life is gone."

Then, suddenly, we are talking so intimately that I am frightened, and want to escape, he saying, "I wonder what good it's been..." and I say, "You've given part of your life to me. Maybe that's all we can ever do with our lives, give some to someone else." And he nods, "Yes, yes, that's it." And I can feel his death which is the last little bit of all the actions we call living, an old man and a young man; and it is intolerable.

So that abruptly he says, "But let's not talk like this. Let's go down in the garden." And he smiles again, and moves off restlessly, and I'm glad to go.

He has trouble to read, and can only do it with labour, and even a book on his desk will be hard to find again once put down. And he asks about England, and about Tomlinson, and tells of how he was put through some tests at Berkeley by some psychologists who were investigating the "creative genius," and grins happily, childishly, "Oh, I gave them their money's worth. Oh, I really put it on. Some of the things I said! Well, they asked for it, so they could have it. I don't care, not any more."

We spoke of Allen Ginsberg and of Cid Corman; and he spoke out of deep feeling and warmth, and pity too, for their struggles. And Floss told of old parties, of Max Bodenheim who came to scrounge off them, and who announced the first evening that he couldn't eat carrots under any circumstances. And she said, "So I made damn sure I served him carrots the very next meal, and he ate them too!" She didn't have much opinion of him, anyway. I could sense that some of WCW's friends, of this kind, had been more than a slight barb between them.

So we talked on, about nothing much, gossip mostly, as if we had been old neighbours… And then we thought of my car, and the parking meter "…I've got a nickel here for the meter. Go on. Go on. They'll catch you if they can."

I remark on a huge boulder, about half my height, standing in the bushes. "Oh, that was dug up when they were putting in the foundations for the place across the street. I asked if I could have it. I don't know why I wanted it. But I got it. They thought I was crazy."

And he looked around at the street, the American small-town street, spacious, with trees and lawns; and in the autumn now, thick with scattered leaves. "It's not my life, but I couldn't get out. I don't know how it could be otherwise. It must be different in England." And I can sense it, and am appalled, that *he* should feel isolated and cut off, he of all people, and I say, "Then indeed, if *you* feel that, if you do, then there is hope for all and any of us." Then he shakes his head, and moves restlessly back to the house, as if to show that he didn't mean me to take him seriously.

We go through where they are rebuilding the new surgery and waiting room for his son. He is at times critical of it, and then unsure. "D'you think the steps are too big? I mean, for mothers with children?"

I can see that he is tired, the strain of a visitor makes him nervous, and we gather ourselves to go. We squeeze their hands, and they hold the children for a moment, and we say all the usual things that one does say, and mean all of them.

He says, "I don't suppose we'll ever see you again. It's always like that. All our friends." And I want to deny it, I want to say, "But of course we'll see you again," and I want to say that we'll be back soon. But I know that what he says is true, that we may quite probably not see each other again, and I drive away very quickly down the main street, seeing the sign "Rutherford" by a bank, to get away, because it's all that I can do not to cry, and that's very stupid somehow.

But, equally, proud that I want to cry. For if there be nothing in life worth such tears, just to say good-bye, then indeed we have nothing. So back into New York, back into the traffic, and the tall buildings, in the early evening, still light, still hearing their voices in our ears, while the taxis crash past, on every side and I wonder if I'll ever be able to find a place to park.

A Gesture to Be Clean
Some Notes on the Poetry of William Carlos Williams

In the American Grain is a series of meditations and speculations on the lives of a number of men who helped to shape America. By trying to understand their experiences Williams looks for clues to orientate himself. But although it is as an American looking at America that he writes, any reader in any country may find the experience relevant. For although these questions are posed more insistently and more crudely in America, they are not peculiar to America. Perhaps for a European living in Europe, they could be even more difficult, because more complex and more insidious.

Williams looks to what has been recorded; but it is not for the sake of history. It is only a means of finding out how others coped with problems similar to his own. One of these men is Edgar Allan Poe. This is not the Poe of whom we usually think—the onomatopoeic poet, or the writer of horror tales. Williams has read to more purpose than that. He finds the clues he seeks in the essays that Poe wrote criticising contemporary literature. Williams senses what Poe was after in these, and writes of it:

> Either the new world must be mine as I will have it, or it is a worthless bog. There can be no concession. His (Poe's) attack was *from the center out*. Either I exist or I do not exist and no amount of pap which I happen to be lapping can dull me to the loss. It was a doctrine, anti-American. Here everything was makeshift, everything colossal, in profusion. The frightened hogs or scared birds feeding on the corn—it left, in 1840, the same mood as ever dominant around us. Take what you can get. What you lack, copy. It was a population stuffed with braggadocio, whom Poe so beautifully summarises in many of his prose tales. To such men, all of them, the most terrible experience in the world is to be shown up. This Poe did, in his criticisms, with venomous accuracy. It was a gesture, to BE CLEAN. It was a wish, to *have* the world, or leave it. It was the truest instinct in America demanding to be satisfied, and an end to makeshifts, self deceptions and grotesque excuses. And yet the grotesque inappropriateness of the life about him forced itself in among his words.[1]

---

[1] By William Carlos Williams: 'Edgar Allan Poe' from *In the American Grain* copyright © 1933 by William Carlos Williams. Reprinted by permission of New Directions Publishing Corp.

"A gesture to be clean". This is one clue upon which Williams seizes; and it is exemplified in so many of the earlier poems, such as this:

> As the cat
> climbed over
> the top of
>
> the jamcloset
> first the right
> forefoot
>
> carefully
> then the hind
> stepped down
>
> into the pit of
> the empty
> flowerpot.[2]

"A gesture to be clean". To have the world as it is, not to dress it up. The things themselves, however absurd, however limited. It is something. It is a start. "An end to makeshifts".

With this poem, and others of the same kind, it is hard to resist asking: "But what does it *mean*? Does it symbolise something? Or is there some aesthetic design in the picture it presents?" And so on. Or else one writes a parody to demonstrate that any fool could write a poem like that, as any fool can.

But for Williams, this sort of poem is not concerned with the visual pattern of a picture, and most emphatically does not symbolise anything, It is intended quite literally. The poem *is* a cat, a jam closet and a flowerpot, no more and no less. The meaning, if one must have a meaning in this sense, lies in the presentation of the physical presence of the objects. The poem says, if one must have it say something more than the words it does say, "Things exist!"

Randall Jarrell has written: "The materials of Williams' unsuccessful poems have as much reality as the brick one stumbles over on the side-

---

[2] By William Carlos Williams, 'Poem' from *The Collected Poems Volume I, 1909-1939*, copyright © 1938 by New Directions Publishing Corp. Reprinted by permission of New Directions Publishing Corp and Carcanet Press.

walk: but how little has been done to them…" It is an apt observation. However, perhaps more apt than just. For indeed, such an effect is but a confirmation of Williams' intention.

It is enlightening to compare what D.H. Lawrence has written about Cézanne, because there is a sense in which Williams in these poems is trying to get at the same thing that Lawrence felt that Cézanne was trying to get at in his paintings:

> The actual fact is that in Cézanne modern French art made its first tiny step (from Impressionist Light) back: to real substance, to objective substance, if we may call it so. Van Gogh's earth was still subjective earth, himself projected in the earth. But Cézanne's apples are a real attempt to let the apple exist in its own separate entity… Cézanne's great effort was, as it were, to shove the apple away from him, and let it live of itself. It seems a small thing to do: and yet it is the first real sign that man has made for several thousands of years that he is willing to admit that matter *actually* exists… It seems little, and he died embittered. But it is the first step that counts, and Cézanne's apple is a great deal more than Plato's Idea.[3]

And so, Williams' "object-poems" may seem a small thing to do: and of course, in a way, they are a small thing to do; and they form only a small part of the body of Williams' poetry. Yet we are mistaken if we flick the pages past them, as being too obvious to deserve attention. It was not beneath Williams' dignity to write them. It took a profoundly stubborn mind to be willing to conceive them as poems. That things exist in their physical presence is not an understanding that anyone can afford to view with contempt.

The first poem in *The Collected Later Poems* is entitled 'A Sort of a Song', but it might equally well be 'A Sort of a Manifesto':

> Let the snake wait under
> his weed
> and the writing
> be of words, slow and quick, sharp
> to strike, quiet to wait,
> sleepless.

---

[3] *Phoenix: The Posthumous Papers of D.H. Lawrence* (London: Heinemann 1936).

> —through metaphor to reconcile
> the people and the stones.
> Compose. (No ideas
> but in things) Invent!
> Saxifrage is my flower that splits
> the rocks.[4]

"No ideas but in things". It is a phrase that he repeats elsewhere, and one that has been misunderstood. It does not slight the importance of ideas. Rather the contrary—that ideas matter so very much that they can only be properly understood in terms as immediate as those in which we see a cat or a jamcloset. Only thus, as he understands Poe, can there be "an end to makeshift".

This is not to be understood in the facile sense of using pictures to illustrate cultural generalisations, like a lecture with lantern slides. Rather it is an effort "...to have the world", all of it; to have the forms which govern our experiences on the same terms as one might recognise a snake under a weed. To "know" the ideas which support the world of men in which one lives, as immediately as one "knows" a chair on which one happens to be sitting.

For Williams, "the writing... of words" and "the snake... under his weed" belong to the same kind of reality. This identity is not achieved by turning the snake into an abstraction, merely a symbolic snake to signify something else in the world of ideas. It must remain a physical snake, under a physical weed, probably at the bottom of his garden. It is a snake that can bite, that can interfere in a man's life, that is beautiful and dangerous. The writing of words, in the same breath, in the same poem (and in our lives, since for Williams, our lives are a kind of poem) must be equally "sharp to strike, quiet to wait, sleepless".

"...to reconcile the people and the stones". It may sound a peculiar ambition. But it is merely that Williams would have us feel at home in the world—as much at home, as inevitable, as a flower growing out of a crack in a rock. It is not a small ambition.

*

---

[4] By William Carlos Williams, from *The Collected Poems: Volume II, 1939-1962*, copyright © 1944 by New Directions Publishing Corp. Reprinted by permission of New Directions Publishing Corp and Carcanet Press.

With this "gesture to be clean" comes the other clue which Williams finds in Poe... the distinction between "nationality in letters", which Poe carefully slights, and the pre-eminent importance, in letters, as in all other branches of imaginative creation, of the *local*...

> What he [Poe] wanted was connected with no particular place: therefore it *must* be where he *was*... What he says, being thoroughly local in origin, has some chance of being universal in application...[5]

This sense of the importance of "the local conditions" is not to be confused with a cultivation of what is merely provincial. To be provincial is to take ideas at second-hand, without proving them for oneself. Nor does the local exalt any particular locality. What it does affirm is that if a man can get his feet on whatever ground happens to be under him, then his experience will partake of what is universal. Just as Poe attacked "from the center out", so Williams would work "from the root up".

Yet a lot of what appears to be local in Williams is only a surface. One could write for ever about one's own back garden, about one's job, or one's neighbours, without ever really penetrating farther than the kind of local colour a tourist might describe. Williams' sense of the local is more than that. These accidents of place (and his place might be any place, one has no more significance than another, in itself) do not serve anything. The poet, as any man, must learn to grasp it on his own terms, in order to make something of it. "To have the world". It begins to come back to the previous necessity, "to be clean". It is what can make sense out of the most trivial happening. And our lives are made up out of such apparent trivia.

To make contact like this, requires resources, of a personal kind. Williams writes, in a poem called 'The Cure':

> Sometimes I envy others, fear them
> a little too, if they write well.
> For when I cannot write I'm a sick man
> and want to die. The cause is plain.

---

[5] By William Carlos Williams from *In the American Grain, op. cit.* Reprinted by permission of New Directions Publishing Corp.

> But they have no access to my sources.
> Let them write then as they may and
> perfect it as they can they will never
> come to the secret of that form
>
> Interknit with the unfathomable ground
> where we walk daily and from which
> among the rest you have sprung
> and opened flowerlike to my hand.[6]

It is his secret, and the strength of his best poetry. Courage might be one word for it. Even when most utterly involved in the details of the life about him, he seems to keep in touch with "...that form interknit with the unfathomable ground where we walk daily..." In a letter to Marianne Moore, he says: "It is something that occurred once when I was about twenty, a sudden resignation to existence, a despair—if you wish to call it that, but a despair which made everything a unit and at the same time a part of myself, I suppose it might be called a sort of nameless religious experience. I resigned. I gave up. I decided there was nothing else in life for me but to work... I won't follow causes. I can't. The reason is that it seems so much more important to me that I am. Where shall one go? What shall one do? Things have no names for me and places have no significance. As a reward for this anonymity I feel as much a part of things as trees and stones."

*

Williams may celebrate his America, but it is no perpetual Fourth of July. If anything, rather the opposite. The local conditions in this instance can be terrifyingly brutal.

> The pure products of America
> go crazy—
> mountain folk from Kentucky
>
> or the ribbed north end of
> Jersey

---

[6] By William Carlos Williams, from *The Collected Poems Volume II 1939-1962*, op. cit. Reprinted by permission of New Directions Publishing Corp and Carcanet Press.

> with its isolate lakes and
> valleys, its deaf-mutes, thieves
> old names,
> and promiscuity between
>
> devil-may-care men who have taken
> to railroading
> out of sheer lust of adventure—
>
> and young slatterns, bathed
> in filth
> from Monday to Saturday
>
> to be tricked out that night
> with gauds
> from imaginations which have no
>
> peasant traditions to give them
> character
> but flutter and flaunt
>
> sheer rags—succumbing without
> emotion
> save numbed terror
>
> under some hedge of choke-cherry
> or viburnum—
> which they cannot express—[7]

The energy and potential exist. The form is lacking. The waste that this implies is appalling. Williams himself does not presume to be exempt. In his autobiography he writes:

> Do we not see that we are inarticulate? That is what defeats us. It is our inability to communicate to one another how we are locked within ourselves unable to say even the simplest thing of importance to one another, any of us, even the most

---

[7] By William Carlos Williams, 'Spring and All' from *Selected Poems*, copyright © 1985 by New Directions Publishing Corp. Reprinted by permission of New Directions Publishing Corp.

valuable, that makes our lives like those of a litter of kittens in a wood-pile...[8]

This is not to be confused with a histrionic gesture to excuse inadequate writing. It is "the railroad men" and "the young slatterns tricked out with gauds" whom he has in mind. Nor is it that such men and women should be able to express themselves as a poet might; but that there should be some means by which they can express something of value to themselves. In the past, and in other cultures, there were traditions and ceremonies, both religious and secular. As Williams sees the men and women of his own city, they have nothing left. Or else they try to imitate forms of expression borrowed from without or from the past which have no relevance to the world in which they live. Nor is the poet exempt, unless he try to deny his situation.

Sometimes too, the potential comes to the surface, and finds whatever means it can force to its will; and the nation or history will not tolerate it. A man can be born in the wrong place at the wrong time. Aaron Burr is such a figure for Williams, a man who came to prominence in the years immediately following the American Revolution In the history books he is shown as a firebrand, a demagogue, a potential Caesar or Buonaparte. Williams does not deny this; but also asserts the other side of the story, and all the great energy of spirit gone for nothing.

> Burr saw America in his imagination, free. His spirit leaped to it—and his body followed out of a sick bed. But his spark was not preserved. He saw America or he had seen America, as a promise of delight and it struck fine earth, that fancy. Now he saw a sombre Washington—with shrewd dog Hamilton at his side—locking the doors, closing the windows, building fences and providing walls. He dreaded this. He saw that they would only lock themselves up and he rebelled.
>
> Inspired by devil or angel, Burr was a frightful danger to the young state and needed to be curbed.

---

[8] By William Carlos Williams, from *The Autobiography of William Carlos Williams* copyright © 1951 by William Carlos Williams. Reprinted by permission of New Directions Publishing Corp.

So much the worse for the young state, then. But it's the malice I decry. Burr's account in history is a distortion. The good which history should have preserved, it tortures. A country is not free, is not what it pretends to be, unless it leave a vantage open (in tradition) for that which Burr possessed in such a remarkable degree.[9]

A good deal of Williams' poetry goes towards asserting just such a vantage, for that kind of spirit. If a tradition cannot accommodate that kind of energy, then it is defective. Tradition. It is not an easy word to use when writing about Williams, yet it is an important one. Williams does assert a tradition; though he sees it as only partly formed, as he looks back to men like Poe or Burr. In the one, he finds clues for his own use; in the other he sees the disaster consequent upon too narrow a tradition.

Thus, Williams himself expends a good deal of effort unlocking doors and knocking down walls. This is expressed not only in his handling of the subject matter of his poems, but in his attitude to the poem as a structure of words. In much of his early poetry there is a frankly destructive emphasis. He appears to break the lines where a reader least expects a break. Often, it is arbitrary. However, it is a way of accomplishing his purpose, which is to find a form which will accommodate just exactly the kind of potential which, as he sees it in the case of Aaron Burr, might otherwise go to waste.

This effort is not directed against the structure of language itself: as, for example, in the work of certain surrealist writers. The destructive effort is directed against the almost mechanical assumptions of the great bulk of inherited English and American poetic usage. It is what gives his poems their staccato, rather breathless effect: a roughness of surface that is at once identifiable.

> Fury and counter fury! The volcano!
> Stand firm, unbending. The chemistry
> shifts. The retort does not fracture.
> The change reveals—change.

---

[9] William Carlos Williams: 'Aaron Burr' from *In the American Grain, op. cit.* Reprinted by permission of New Directions Publishing Corp.

The revelation is compact—
compact of regathered fury

By violence lost, recaptured by violence
violence alone opens the shell of the nut.
The best is hard to say—unless
near the break. Unless the shell hold
the kernel is not sweet.
Under violence the meat lies regained

Each age brings new calls upon violence
for new rewards, variants of the old.
Unless each hold firm
Unless each remain flexible
there can be no new. The new opens
new ways beyond all known ways.

Shut up! laughs the big she-Wop.
Wait till you have six like me.
Every year one. Come on! Push! Sure.
you said it! Maybe I have one next year.
Sweating like a volcano. It cleans you up,
makes you feel good inside. Come on! Push![10]

In much of this, Williams has been badly served by his followers. It is only too easy to copy some of his mannerisms, without any specific sense of the need which has induced them. To quote Lawrence again, writing about Cézanne:

> ...The fight with the cliché is the most obvious thing in his pictures. The dust of battle rises thick, and the splinters fly wildly. And it is this dust of battle and flying of splinters which his imitators still so fervently imitate... He let off various explosions in order to blow up the stronghold of the cliché, and his followers make grand firework imitations of the explosions, without the faintest inkling of the true attack.

---

[10] William Carlos Williams, 'Catastrophic Birth' in *The Collected Poems Volume II 1939-1962, op. cit.* Reprinted by permission of New Directions Publishing Corp and Carcanet Press.

More Words

Some of Williams' contemporaries and avowed followers have written from an exclusively and merely destructive point of view. They hated the sonnet (I use the sonnet as a convenient example, as Williams does, and they have) because they could not endure its perfection. Williams attacked because he wanted its perfection—but on his own terms.

From a Notebook: A Speculation

Surely the whole point about "form" in poetry is not that of discipline; that is, not in the sense of some restrictive obstacle against which or within which one has to work. (As if there were any virtue in merely learning to flex one's muscles.)

How often one hears the complaint that the modern poet has it too easy, doesn't really have to work at his poem. (As if there was some sort of value in doing something the hard way. As if form in poetry was some sort of handicap to make the race more complicated.)

The form of a poem must be of positive use. (And I use the word form here in its most obvious and crude sense as a verbal device or diagram.) It may be that its function happens more in the making of the poem than in the actual reading of it. (Most people read most metrical/rhymed poems as if they were straight prose. In fact, if you read the poem to them even moderately accentuating the metrical/rhyme pattern they will think you are trying to be naive.)

It is true that there is a certain musical value to the traditional forms. They do *sing* to some extent; and I understand that they originally developed under circumstances in which they were sung. This hardly seems a major concern anymore. Experiments in putting poetry back in the direction of music have not been very promising. The *pure poetry of sound* has only demonstrated what was obvious, that pure sound (e.g., music itself) need not worry about the competition from words or syllables. If we want music, we don't want gobbledygook.

Where the sonnet has the advantage over the form of an early poem of Williams is that as one writes it, the necessities of the metric/rhyme pattern actually help to suggest the ideas. The final result, starting from whatever you wish (either a complex idea or merely a first line) will never be entirely what we expected. It will never be merely what we first projected that the poem might contain. The rhymes, especially, will actively suggest and select certain turns of language, and with this, ideas. The form here is actually working in favour of the poet (though he may curse to try to make it adhere exactly to his original intent.)

In contrast, the Williams poem suggests nothing, selects nothing. The poet has to supply everything himself—everything. When it comes down to it, it is a much harder form in which to write something that is verbally and conceptually interesting.

Not that form of course, is merely a matter of metric/rhyme scheme. Far from it. There are conventions (which formally direct a poem) which are much harder to define. The best way to express them is often by a parody. A certain poet develops a style which is so distinct that it can be applied to any subject (as in the parody, with hilarious results). Nonetheless, for the poet who has found it, *his* form acts to help him write his poems. The conditions under which he allows himself to use his language affect his ideas and verbal expressions as strongly as can rhyme and meter. And in his best poems this will work toward producing a final result which he may scarcely have anticipated. Hence, the common notion of "The Muse dictated the poem to me." What this means is: I have learned a certain form so well that the poem wrote itself.

Form, taken to this extreme, comes much closer to what one usually means by style or personality. It is what makes a quatrain by Poet *A* vividly different from a quatrain by Poet *B,* though they both make the same statement.

Assuming, then, that (1) Williams is right in saying that the old forms have exhausted themselves or can no longer really help us if our poems are to have an active relationship to the kind of world we live in; and that (2) his own experiments are still only a kind of dressed up *vers libre*, then what we must work toward is a regular pattern upon which a poem can be based and which will dictate rigidly that certain words, or certain phrases, or certain grammatical constructions, that these MUST appear at certain places in the sequence—a pattern which will require us to re-arrange our language and employ words which, left to our own choice, would never have occurred to us. The form thus must both suggest and at times even dictate the actual words and their actual sequence as we put the poem together. That it should be difficult or require a lot of skill in order to use this form may be true, but need not be.

Il Miglior Fabbro
or Maybe the Compass Needle Yearns Toward the South

I first came across Pound's Arnault Daniel versions sometime about 1949, probably in a contemporary magazine. I didn't make a note of source but copied a number into my notebook, with samples of the originals.

They made an enormous impact and I have kept them in my mind ever since, even gone back to reread occasionally, as one of the landmark essentials. Fair enough, not the only one, but a basic one. Two of the verses, some other fragments, I found lodged in my memory, almost without effort, and which I still recite to myself.

So that I was considerably startled, in fact challenged, when I read your comment! Enough that I tracked down a copy of the Faber *Translations*, wondering where the discrepancy was, and why. How had I gone wrong? Or had I?

Reading Kenner's Introduction was interesting. He focuses on 'The Seafarer', the 'Cathay' poems, the 'Propertius'. These are the "Make It New" translations, the ones that are part of the accepted Pound collected poems, that can stand as poems in isolation, as remakings into English. No apologies or explanations needed. But the Cavalcanti, the Arnault? Eloquent silence from Kenner. Aha, these don't fit?

So what did the G.T. of 1949 register, even still registers in 1996? The diction is archaic to the point of comedy. There are occasional words twisted out of meaning or grafted with a tense that it is difficult to believe anyone has ever used except the *fabbro* himself ("mearing" for example, as a present participle, from an alternative spelling of "to mere": to set a boundary, make a limit).

What the versions say, express, is conventional enough. Perhaps sometimes there are ambiguities, as if it were all a code or cryptogram for something probably not worth chasing after? A syntax so tortuous that you can gloss as you wish? Ingenuity for its own sake?

All this and yet… and yet… not what Pound was concerned to try to reproduce, which was the pattern of sound and rhythm. And which is what came across so strongly then, and with such force of originality, as something I had not encountered in English verse. Perhaps more of Arnault, less of Pound? Perhaps commonplace enough for anyone familiar with the Provençal lyrical tradition?

Not in all of them so successful of course, but when it succeeded, and still does, miraculous. Particularly verses three and four of 'Chan chai la fueilla':

> Aye, life's a high thing,
>   where joy's his maintenance,
> Who cries 'tis wry thing
>   hath danced never my dance,
> I can advance
>   no blame against fate's tithing
> For lot and chance
>   have deemed the best thing, my thing.
>
> Of love's wayfaring
>   I know no part to blame,
> All other paring,
>   compared, is put to shame,
> Man can acclaim
>   no second for comparing
> With her, no dame
>   but hath the meaner bearing.[1]

The shift in the caesura between the first pairs of lines and the second, plus the completely interlocking rhyme scheme, I find quite an extraordinary technical feat, and he sustains it with hardly a falter, for seven stanzas and a coda.

Perhaps there are others who have reproduced the music of Arnault more successfully, or more fluently? I should be delighted to read them! There are a few places where even his invention sags and he skips or fudges. Maybe I'll try myself?

---

[1] This translation, originally intended for a book of translations of Arnault Daniel in 1917, appeared in the essay 'Arnault Daniel' in *Instigations* (New York: Boni and Liveright 1920), and subsequently in *Translations* (New York: New Directions 1963) and *Poems & Translations*, ed. Richard Sieburth (New York: The Library of America 2003).

Some Notes on *The Maximus Poems* of Charles Olson

There are poems about which it is easy to say, "It says so-and-so" or "The point of it is such-and-such". There are other poems which aren't so easily grasped because there is no final statement which can be summarised. If you like, they don't state so much as indicate possibilities. They don't arrive so much as move towards. Nor is it slighting to say of them that the writer himself does not always know towards what they move. Because a journey has no destination that can be labelled beforehand doesn't mean that the journey has no purpose. I think that *The Maximus Poems* can be considered in some such way.

They are in the form of letters written by Olson to his native town of Gloucester, a seaport in New England. He remembers some of his own life there, and the lives of others he knew, chiefly men of the fishing fleets. He goes back into history, to the men who first explored that coast, and even to their native England. He speaks to and of them all, the living and the dead, and tries to find some base on which he can stand and from which he can start. In a sense, these are poems concerned with finding a place and a context from which he can start to write.

> I measure my song,
> measure the sources of my song,
> measure me, measure
> my forces

What holds it together? Superficially in their structure they have resemblances to the *Cantos* and perhaps even more to *Paterson*. The places and people and comments shift rapidly, often in the middle of a sentence. Certain names and themes recur, and occasionally he refers to personal memories. It isn't easy reading.

>   Gloucester, your first house was as Elizabeth's
> England
>
> (and that that Endecott, the "New" should have used it
> inside of which to smile, and bless that covenant Higginson and
>   the others…

It sat
where my own house has been (where I am
founded

It is a commonplace that poetry of this sort is rarely successful. There have been enough feeble imitators to prejudice us against it. And in the last few years there has been a widespread return to the traditional disciplines of formal rhyme and meter. I think that the key word here is *discipline*. We look for necessity in poetry, for a sense that the language is being used according to some structure, that the vocal cords are drawn taut to some purpose.

The necessity, or *form* of *The Maximus Poems* is the concern of the writer, *concern* in itself, the concern that he must find words, must find what needs to be said. Without rhyme or formal meter or any such devices, I believe that *The Maximus Poems* have all the urgency and pattern that can be found in, say, 'The Wreck of the Deutschland'. In *Maximus*, it is an inner compulsion, not an external one. Yet, after all, the external pattern of Hopkins is merely the surface reflection of the inner form, which is that of a man saying what he must in the only way that he can. It is this sense of the inevitable—that within the framework of the poem, the language could not possibly be other than it is—that strikes me as what is important.

The Maximus Poems, 1–10, 11–22. Beautiful 12"x9" format. $3.00 each from the publisher, Jonathan Williams, Box 344, Highlands, NC, U.S.A.[1]

---

[1] Since republished in *The Maximus Poems*, ed. George F. Butterick (Berkeley: University of California Press 1983).

Left: Charles Olson, Vancouver, 1963. Photo by Gael Turnbull [?].

Below: Gael Turnbull with Cid Corman, Ventura, CA, 1961. Photo by Jonnie Turnbull.

Cid Corman

>   to the little something
>   at the centre

Many of the poems in this collection[1] are, it is true, in structure simply imagist or haiku—one is an affectionate echo of Williams' "As the cat / climbed over etc". But one at least achieves what seems to me a remarkable breakthrough:

>   I picked a
>   leaf up
>
>   it weighed
>   my vision
>
>   I knelt and
>   placed it
>
>   almost
>   where it was

The pivotal effect of the one word "almost", enough to retrieve the abstraction of "weighed my vision", brings the whole poem to life. It is also one of the first to be written to a strict syllabic count (yet with variation of pace) which I think proves to be one of the most successful devices in Corman's later poetry.

By the time of *For Instance* (published early 1962, dated November 1961) he had further defined and developed this characteristic type of poem. There are still many in general style imitations of the haiku but ranging away from the conventions of that form into other possibilities. There is the technical delight of such as this, again using the syllable count to great effect:

---

[1] It is unclear exactly which of Corman's many publications this piece refers to. The poem 'I picked a / leaf up…' was however first published in *For Sure* (Kyoto: Origin Press 1960) and subsequently republished on many occasions, including an appearance as a poster on the buses, before appearing again in Corman's *OF*, Vol. 1 (Venice, CA: Lapis Press 1990).

> green tree
> over gray rock
> shadow of tree
> over shadow
> of rock
>
> sit here
> in the sunlight
> out of it all
> before going
> on in

The link here with the haiku is clear but the particular language of the last three lines seems unique with its play on words exploring meaning and joining in the play. Another poem from this collection is:

> blown against pane
> against sky
> a bee
>
> the train stops then
> pulls on for
> all time
>
> I was going
> to say I
> am here

The first two stanzas might be just another imagist/haiku type of poem except for the enigmatic "all time", as it then shifts into something else but without forcing the reader to make any more connection between the last stanza and the first two than he or she may wish. There is also the play of the balance between "I was going" and "I am here".

The final epigraph to this little collection is also characteristic:

> when every word listens
> silence sings to itself

This is not obviously Japanese in the means of its expression and what it actually *means* might be dubious to try to explain or justify but that is not the point. He had found a shape of language which is startling in how far it is from that of the poems he was publishing even two years before.

It is true that there may have been a delayed influence of Zukofsky whom he had known personally and whose poems he had published and championed since at least 1957. He had also been translating widely in other languages and reading omnivorously. However, the textual evidence is that it was the experience of translating Japanese poetry (initially at least with Kamaike Susumu) which provided the catalytic insight.

When he came to put together *In Good Time* in 1964, there was much from which he could choose and he certainly included a few of the early poems but only those which are near in technique to those of *For Sure, For Instance* and some subsequent collections. The arrangement is into five sections. He was to develop this later, shifting the focus of the categories. Here it is by place.

Thus the poems 'An Orthodoxy', 'The Overpass', 'The Sill', taken from early pamphlets are under *Boston* with poems which in technique appear to be much later or to have been reworked, such as the syllabic 'D-Day V-Letter,' or the non-syllabic 'Deceased' with its gentle inversions of phrase, again so much part of his post 1959/1960 work:

> there was
> much to tell you
>
> now there is nothing
> to say

His own comment on his poems tends to ignore technique as if all that was needed was a purity of vision. But a proportional purity of language had to be found as well.

I have tried to indicate here something of the process by which after many years of writing, Corman found such a means. Yet to say *found* might suggest that it was gratuitous. Such discoveries are only realized by those who search and are capable of recognizing their relevance when chance and toil may present.

Some Notes on the Poetry of Robert Duncan

To understand? To stand under. Not sit or kneel, but stand. Fully upright and yet beneath. As we may, and do.

Not that we may be very sure, very often, how much we understand.

"Let the writing be of words" wrote William Carlos Williams. And for Duncan, there is that very special sense in which it is. Where he makes his *hommage* to Gertrude Stein (see: *Writing Writing*, Sum Books, Albuquerque).

That the meaning of a word should be not merely in what we *understand* from it, but in the sound itself. And in the sign. A sign: to signal. A sound: to plumb, to let down the lead, to find what depth.

And so, navigation. Sightings and bearings. All these. Or thereabouts. To be understood not as approximate but as exact. As that area adjacent to a place, as to what surrounds and relates to what *is* there. As absolute.

To muse. Upon a muse. For amusement. Amazement. In a maze. For the maize, we feed upon. A God, that nourishes! That sustains the Spirit.

> There where great Artemis rides
> naked, lake-clear bright lady
> awakening her lovers, the hunters
>   and the hunted,
> her horns sound in the night.
>
> Or are they horns of distant cars?
> themselves fading and yet insistent,
> [...]
> We are awake now indeed,
> and we are her Kings...[1]

---

[1] By Robert Duncan, from 'The Horns of Artemis', from *Selected Poems*, copyright © 1950 by Robert Duncan, Reprinted by permission of New Directions Publishing Corp.

More Words

But not by contrivance. The words invoke, not command us. (Though they may command the Poet) It must happen. It cannot be made to happen. (But sloth has no part with it.)

>Neither our vices nor our virtues
further the poem. "They came up
>   and died
just like they do every year
>   on the rocks."

>The poem
feeds upon thought, feeling, impulse,
>   to breed   itself,
a spiritual urgency at the dark ladders leaping.

>This beauty is an inner persistence
>   toward the source
striving against (within) down-rushet of the river,
>   a call we heard and answer…[2]

There is a remark quoted on the jacket of *The Opening of the Field* (Grove Press): "I make poetry as other men make war or make love or make states or revolutions: to exercise my faculties at large."

>You are right. What we call Poetry is the boat.
The first boat, the body—but it was a bed.
>   The bed, but it was a car.
And the driver or sandman, the boatman,
>   the familiar stranger, first lover,
is not with me.

>   You are wrong.
What we call Poetry is the lake itself,
the bewildering circling water way—
having our power in what we know nothing of…[3]

---

[2] By Robert Duncan, from 'Poetry, A Natural Thing', from *The Opening of the Field*, copyright © 1960 by Robert Duncan. Reprinted by permission of New Directions Publishing Corp.

[3] By Robert Duncan, from 'A New Poem (for Jack Spicer)', from *Roots and Branches*, copyright © 1964 by Robert Duncan. Reprinted by permission of New Directions Publishing Corp.

Some Notes on the Poetry of Robert Duncan

Robert Duncan, May 1956. Photo by Jonnie Turnbull.

Continual, the reach for what is Beyond. And the willingness to submit to it. As equally, the conviction that what is Known cannot be taken from us. Cannot, with impunity, be slighted. In a recent pamphlet (*As Testimony*, White Rabbit Press, San Francisco) he says: "Well, I have my obsessions; and where my spirit feeds, where there is that other mystery of orders that I find in poetry, I am a fanatic not an aesthete. I can no more adjust myself to like or dislike here than I can appreciate the universe. I am in-bound to the event and suffer with the event in its disregard. I cannot get the perspective where there are levels shifting that these are effects or devices only..." Again, elsewhere, he has declared: "It is not expression nor creation that I seek; but my inventions are addressed to an adventure."

> To throw a window open
> upon the marges of a sea!
>
> In the closed room
> when the party was going
> we heard the ocean
> out there.

More Words

> "Look out there!"
> the old man warnd the young lords.
> "Do not look out there.
>
> "Yesterday is talking upon its sands.
> Let it talk on. Do not
>
> look out upon that land
> for it is all water
>   and washes the shores of this land away."[4]

In an essay (in *Kulchur* 4) Duncan quotes (with his always refreshing range of perception and sympathy) from Carlyle: "All deep things are Song. It seems somehow the very central essence of us, Song; as if all the rest were but wrappages and hulls! The primal element of us; and of all things. The Greeks fabled of Sphere-Harmonies: it was the feeling they had of the inner structure of Nature; that the soul of all her voices and utterances was perfect music. Poetry, therefore, we call musical thought, The Poet is he who thinks in that manner. At bottom, it turns still on power of intellect; it is a man's sincerity and depth of vision that make him a Poet…"

> How the Earth turns round under the Sun I know,
> And how the Numbers in the Constellations glow,
> How all Forms in Time will grow
> And return to their single Source
> Informd by Grief, Joy, insatiable Desire
> And cold Remorse.
>
> Serpents I have seen bend the Evening Air
> Where Flowers that once Men and Women were
> Voiceless spread their innocent Lustre.
> I have seen green Globes of Water
> Enter the Fire. In my Sight
> Tears have drownd the Flames of Animal Delight.[5]

---

[4] from 'From *The Mabinogion*', in *Roots and Branches*, op. cit. Reprinted by permission of New Directions Publishing Corp.
[5] from 'The Ballad of the Enamord Mage' in *The Opening of the Field*, op.cit. Reprinted by permission of New Directions Publishing Corp.

There are, of course, many poems where the rhetoric appears to shed its radiance inwards, instead of out. It is part of Duncan's *hommage* and submission to his language. Say but one word, and perhaps one has already said too much. Duncan observes: "A man writes 'I love' on a wall. He hopes to escape from his mistake by not signing his name. But a glamour radiates from the letters and has illuminated his being as he writes… The man, if he sees or hears at all, is violently alterd then, revolted by disowning what he was. He has contradicted himself, spoken his unspoken self; and transferrd the power from what he might have declared to what he has declared." Though its concerns may often seem far, for many readers, the richness and the fertility are always near.

> If I think of my element, it is not fire,
> of ember and ash, but of earth,
> nor of man's travail and burden
> to work in the dirt, but of the abundance,
> the verdant rhetorical…
> …
> robed round in sound, rich as a tree
> in full foliage of metaphor, flower and fruit.[6]

In an essay in *Black Mountain Review* he cautions; "Blake pays no attention to the beautiful. He desires the joyous… For, though Blake is beautiful, the beauty is a by-product of his desire, and, at his very best, of his joyousness. Though he does not desire elegance, his intensity renders him distinctive, and his work can become the artifact of an elegant mind. Such are the ironies of our endeavours." Thus, one hesitates to single out this or that poem as particularly supreme as a poem. Yet, for myself, there are many that have just this sort of finished achievement. That are radiant, even in isolation. In particular: 'Often I Am Permitted to Return to a Meadow', 'This Place Rumord to Have Been Sodom', and 'Food for Fire, Food for Thought' (from *The Opening of the Field*); 'Roots and Branches', 'Come Let Me Free Myself', 'Arethusa' (a *tour de force* of rhyme and rhythm) 'Sonnet One', (from *Roots and Branches*) and of the earlier poems especially: 'Song of the Border Guard' and 'Processionals'.

---

[6] from 'Returning to the Rhetoric of an Early Mode' from *Roots and Branches*, op. cit. Reprinted by permission of New Directions Publishing Corp.

More Words

"He desires the joyous." Again and again in Duncan's poems the primacy of pleasure is asserted. And indeed that very pleasure which beckons to us from childhood. A warmth of blood. A delight.

> You have carried a branch of tomorrow into the room.
> Its fragrance has awakend me—no,
>
>> it was the sound of a fire on the hearth
>
>> leapd up where you bankd it, sparks of delight.
>>   Now I return the thought
>
>> to the red glow, that might-be-magical blood,
>> palaces of heat in the fire's mouth
>
> "If you look you will see the salamander,"
>
>> to the very elements that attend us,
>> fairies of the fire, the radiant crawling…
>
> That was a long time ago.
> No, they were never really there,
>
>> tho once I saw—Did I stare
>> into the heart of desire burning
>> and see a radiant man? like those
>> fancy cities from fire into fire falling?
>
> We are close enough to childhood, so easily purged
> of whatever we thought we were to be,
>
>> flamey threads of firstness go out from your touch.
>
>> Flickers of unlikely heat
>> at the edge of our belief bud forth.[7]

---

[7] from 'Food for Fire, Food for Thought,' from *The Opening of the Field*, op. cit. Reprinted by permission of New Directions Publishing Corp.

From a Journal, 9 February, 1958

Ginsberg—Two days. Hair thinning on top—Body odour (unchanged underwear)—Nicotine fingers, thick glasses—sensual, almost liver lips—"crazy mixed up kid"—his catch phrase "hung up"—reading "I am with you in Rockland" in long breathless monotone, to set my mind back to church, to the priest reciting in a Jewish Orthodox service, until I had to say "Amen" after each, half mocking, half serious—his gingivitis bleeding, and his worry over it, his gums receding—to see a lamb in a green field (Blake)—and to see the dark satanic mills—peyote, Yage, LSD 6 and LSD 12—trudging through the wet snow, slipping and falling, in the mist, to stand where the wind groaned in the trees over the ancient camp [on the Malvern hills], forgotten wars—what will become of him? I was almost reluctant to let him go—his dream (on the cathedral tower) of being on the top of a tower, with no stairs down—called Rexroth "W.C. Fields"—poem to his mother just dead, refrain, "don't want to…"

(from left to right: Michael Shayer, Allen Ginsberg, Gael Turnbull, Anselm Hollo, at Bridge House, 1965.) Photo by Jonnie Turnbull.

William Burroughs. Drawing by Gael Turnbull, 1957.

Paris and Bill Burroughs

Extracts from a journal, 1958

July 31, 2:30 p.m. Gregory wasn't in his room, though the landlady declared that he usually slept until noon, so he left a note in the door. Incredible sort of little attic under the roof, to get to which one has almost to crawl on hands and feet around the last little spiral turn—so I knocked on the door of this other friend of Ginsberg's, called Bill Burroughs—he only just up, in pyjamas, looking like a man dying of cancer, thin, pale, unsteady, the curtains still drawn—he made some tea, and we exchanged the usual greetings—and he told me the news, that Gregory was going to Lapland, with some explorer he had met only yesterday—then, as we finished our tea, and Burroughs dressed, an older man, about 40, I'd say, very slow speaker—two themes in his talk, a hatred of America, the physical culture of it, and also an interest in all forms of drugs of all kinds—eventually monotonous, but despite this, a rather pathetic sort of sad stick, one couldn't help liking him—Gregory[1] came in, small, a monkey grin of an Italian face, restless almost aggressive at times, under pressure, dynamic, black curly hair and burning black eyes, a face of a faun, something elemental and Mediterranean, in a miniature bouncing sort of way—not really Puck nor really Pan, neither comparison fits, and yet one wants to make one—much, indeed, how I would imagine a mixture of Poe and Villon—in some excitement partly repressed over the trip to Sweden, apologetic to me for leaving as I came, but it was quite obvious to me that he had to go as he had to breathe—walking back and forth, up and down the room—every now and then, grinning in spontaneous friendship like a street urchin—then intent again, off to the North Pole to write a poem that would melt all the icebergs—So he wanted me to take *his* room while he was gone, and took me up to see it—the walls covered very beautifully with colored picture postcard prints, a bit like a stamp collection except that the result was more of a mosaic of Baghdad—he has a black cloak with a royal blue silk lining to it, and a silver headed staff, very priestly indeed, very much the Druid chanter, or a pixie pretending to be one—sometimes his face is cruel, an intensity, that nothing should stop him—speaking

---

[1] Gregory Corso (1930-2001), beat poet.

More Words

of Michaux[2] and various people—then about Kerouac's book which he disliked (though admitting the talent) because of the aesthetic wonder-working vision of America (e.g. Wolfe, Whitman, Dreiser) which he believed false, and wrong—obviously, America was more than that—and then on to W.C.W., belittling him on recent re-reading because he didn't *say* anything—Gregory's recent poem about the H-bomb is shaped like the mushroom cloud—to be printed locally on a broadsheet—very much contemptuous of Kerouac's poems, believing that *Howl* is the great liberating work—smoking occasionally, occasionally breaking off conversation to turn his back on us and pet the cat—obviously a little pleased at the accolade Michaux has paid him—says Michaux was very "proper" and not at all bohemian—they had talked of mescalin mostly—in fact, he hasn't even read any of Michaux's poems—and so down the twisting stair to see the landlady, but she refuses, very much the suspicious concierge, and to our common regret, I have to check in at a hotel around the corner, far too expensive really, so I'll probably only stay three days—and then at lunch time, back to Burroughs' room for a meal of mince and green peppers and tomatoes with them and Gregory's girl, Jane something—a French girl, a model, very much the thin arms and legs sort of doll, very pretty indeed, and smelling very much of success (financial) to whom Gregory was an adorable new pet and toy—another chap also appeared, an American Jew, Graham, and they talked, teasing Gregory about what would happen to him in Lapland, and that the airplane would crash, etc, etc., great humour—until everyone had to go, goodbye, a hand-shake, and a few books of his for me to read—and gone, gone, off to the north, on the back of the wind, I expect—leaving me with Burroughs who insisted on talking about curare and anti-cancer drugs until I excused myself and came back to my room at the hotel—dizzy, dazed, disappointed—though indeed, it was no more than I might have expected—leaving me essentially alone here, to find my own diversion, as best I can—somehow, I doubt if Burroughs ever goes out of his room except to buy food (he says he goes to India in September, just to live, for interest).

---

[2] Henri Michaux (1899-1984), French poet.

August 1, 4 p.m. Went to see Burroughs, and had more tea with him, he must consume as much tea as Dr. Johnson is said to have drunk, and he talked about life in Amazon jungle, the only necessity, modern medical supplies—then we walked out to find a bookshop run by friends of Gregory, but it was still closed (hours of business tend to be 2 p.m. to midnight)…

August 1, Midnight… so, on the crowded Metro, people, starting home from work, like any crowd going home from work—back to my room here, to spray the drawings, and then out to buy some meat and spaghetti and tomato, etc., to make our usual recipe in Burroughs' room—fortunately it turned out successfully, even the red pepper I used instead of chili—with peaches for dessert, and more tea, endless cups of tea, while Burroughs talked on and on, one somehow doesn't think of him as "Bill" but by his last name—then we went out and walked about—I begin to like him, he is pathetic enough, and harmless except to himself—he takes paregoric, which has a slight opium content, and has scoured every drugstore in Paris for it—but I can't recall what we talked about—had coffee somewhere—poor old Burroughs, he has some small private income, and has lived everywhere, Tangier, Mexico, Istanbul—we met some friends of his in an English bookshop, but not anyone of much interest—I note what an impact Gregory and Allen have made, their names are common currency—back here late, and tired, and rather contented, as if some of my curiosity has been assuaged now—as if I had been able to verify what I had known already—that most of the people in the world, and in Paris, are just like you and I, if not more so—as afraid, as monotonous, as rarely of any splendour—despite which, once one forgets that, this is a good place to live, especially on holiday, especially for doing nothing much, especially if you have some money to spend—especially too, if you have a woman, someone to kiss and love—not like poor Burroughs, so shrivelled up and sad, his own wife died years ago, and now he is too stunted, too frozen inside—but he *can* smile, he *can* laugh, I have seen it, though it's an effort—it was almost worth the evening to see him laugh spontaneously—I was telling him something about English class consciousness—that did it!

More Words

August 2, 10:30 p.m. ...a few minutes walk, to the Seine again, and the queer seclusion of the banks, very quiet, very lazy, very intimate, very much the reverse of all the pomp and Napoleonic thunder (and the French kings too, he was the last of them)—very much the Paris, by the river, of lovers and painters and idlers—so on the metro, back to Burroughs, where I made up the rest of the spaghetti, and we drank some red wine with it, and talked—he has met Auden, in New York, and imitated his mincing priggish way of talking—said what a petty tyrant he is, one goes to listen to the master, but isn't allowed to interrupt—told me about Chester Kallman, Auden's boyfriend, a young Jew of only 15 when Auden picked him up—and on, and on, poor old Burroughs who takes opium which he extracts himself from paregoric with great labour—says he's been to nearly every pharmacy in Paris to buy it—now I had a headache, and my legs a bit sore, and two young chaps came in to see Burroughs who were apparently addicts, but pitifully young and quite empty-headed—so I left, to take a brief walk but feeling lonely...

...to Burroughs' room—but he is in a bad mood, I can tell, because he has taken an extra dose of opium to deaden the pain in his heart, and his face is a mask, sunken, his speech maddeningly slow—he talks of his theory of addiction of a biological requirement—and of how there is no boredom under opium, one can't feel bored, because boredom arrives from undischarged tension, and when the tension is cut off there is contentment—he says he has sat looking at his shoe for several hours at a time, quite content—and we expect a visitor, Allen Auson, a wealthy literary dilettante from Venice, American, but he doesn't come—so B. goes out to shop, a last meal, scrambled eggs and the peaches with real heavy almost putty-like rich cream, and red wine, and *biscottes*, how very good, a feast indeed—and B. begins to warm up now, he even smiles, and is gay in a risqué sort of oblique manner, I can tell that he *has* enjoyed my visit, has even felt a little warmth in his heart—I try to draw him, but not much luck with it—hurry, hurry, or I'll miss my train—Ah, so, farewell—good luck, it's been good, so, perhaps we'll see each other again—an awkward handclasp, how trivial the handclasp is, how much better to kiss, a David and Jonathan would have kissed—he, gaunt, grinning in a silly way, waving with one arm like a mechanical soldier—goodbye, goodbye.

Laura Riding: First Awakenings[1]

There are the poems which a poet may write and publish; there are her or his intentions and ideas about the poems, both in anticipation and retrospect; and then there are the responses of readers, even uses to which those poems may be put, perhaps in strange and unexpected ways and long after their maker's death. This book offers some clarification as well as further complication in regard to this process in the case of Laura Riding and her own assessment of poetry in general and her own work in particular.

As is well known, after publishing her *Collected Poems* in 1938—reprinted by Carcanet in 1980—she stopped writing poems and devoted herself to other forms of expression. Her explanation for this is explicit enough and may be distinguished into two inter-related statements.

One, that the *Collected Poems* achieved in its totality something beyond anything which the individual poems achieved, to the extent that individual poems could not have any validity (or at least, any that satisfied her) in isolation. Hence her consistent refusal to have individual poems in anthologies. She did however prepare a *Selected Poems* in 1970, which she considered a valid condensation of the *Collected*.

Secondly, that in this totality she had taken the process of poetry as far as it was possible to take it, and that this was not far enough, or at least seriously deficient; and that this was not due to any failure on her part but a limitation in the nature of poetry itself.

So far as I understand her, by *poetry* she meant not just a particular use of language but both a way of understanding and a way of shaping the experience of being alive, not passive but active, although not in a political or social sense.

Her *Collected Poems* apparently omitted some 200 or so early poems (many of which had been published in magazines) composed prior to 1926 (when she left New York for England). These were left with a friend and rediscovered in 1979. The volume as now published is a carefully edited version of that collection, put together while Laura Riding (by then Laura Jackson) was still alive and given her imprimatur with an 'Author's Preface'.

---

[1] Review of Laura Riding *First Awakening. The Early Poems* edited by Elizabeth Friedmann, Alan J. Clark and Robert Nye (Manchester: Carcanet Press 1992).

There is one detail worth noting: that the collection (from 1925) originally contained 26 poems which were later included "in some form in the *Collected Poems* of 1938" and these, in whatever original form, are omitted (although their titles are listed in an Appendix). This precludes any curiosity, scholarly or otherwise, in regard to any rewriting which may have occurred.

This decision is consistent with the 'Author's Preface' in which she castigates "critical historicizing over poetic texts," and reaffirms the *Collected Poems* as a "self-determining canon ... gathered into finality" and a "collected representation of my progression in the path of the poetic possibilities of ... eloquence." What the statement does not make clear, is what function this publication of the early poems, excluded from that "self-determining canon," is meant to have in relation to that "canon." Her intentions and assessments are certainly of interest and must be respected; but in publishing she has made her poems available and readers may take what interest they choose, even in individual poems. For myself, I find many of them intensely engaging and for their qualities of language (or in her terms, those "possibilities... of eloquence") while finding myself unable to appreciate that "self-determining canon," which appears to be the relationship of the individual poems to each other and to their totality.

However, wider assessment of her work is not immediately relevant to a review of a book such as this which perhaps inevitably contains a great deal which appears dated, if no obvious juvenilia. At the same time, there is work, sometimes just lines, which anticipate a tone and use of expression, even themes, more familiar in the *Collected Poems*. As an almost random example, on p. 209, the one line:

It is a secret not for speaking

rings to my ear as if from her later work but the opening lines of that particular poem begin:

Can lips be laid aside
As they were pipes out-played...?

which seems poetical in a much too obvious and superficial way.

Thus, for the general reader, or even student or writer, I think it would be better to go to the later definitive collection, or the *Selected*. But in spite of her own cautions, for anyone interested in how she came to write the *Collected Poems*, whether as a total "canon" or as individual poems, it would be an invaluable text.

There is also, reprinted in an Appendix, a long statement entitled 'A Prophecy or a Plea' (from 1925) which contains passages which clearly foreshadow some of her later preoccupations and in particular her belief, then unshaken, in the central position of poetry.

Attempts to summarise are always invidious but perhaps excused in a review. In her 'Plea' she assails her contemporaries, however modern in style, as well as traditional writers (although with a generous acknowledgment to Whitman as a near exception) for their passive and not active relationship to life, the mere taking of what experience brings to us and rearranging or transmitting to create no more than "…temporary havens which constitute the notion of beauty"; and especially "The tradition of art, of poetry … as a catharsis…"

She pleads for "outsight" as against "insight," for an "inductive" use of "the poetic mind," not a "deductive." It is also, as she labels the piece, *a prophecy*, and many of the statements and arguments have a slightly excessive tone, and occasionally something of those poetic conventions she attacks.

But there are passages which have a more authentic quality, anticipating a later Laura Riding. "His [her envisioned poet's] poetry may be less pleasant than that which came before it, but it will at any rate be more honest since he must prove it workable at least for him." She ends with a statement, almost indeed more prophetic than perhaps she knew at the time: "If this voyage reveals a futility, it is a futility worth facing."

At one point, admitting the obstacles and limitations, she remarks: "In the meantime a few brave singers will go on singing *quand même.*" For someone who finds many of her individual poems remarkable and fascination in the quality of their eloquence, it is a matter for regret that after 1938, whatever the limitations of that use of language we may label *poetry*, she did not "…go on singing *quand même.*"

The Selected Poems of Raymond Souster[1]

Dear Ray:
          They've asked me to review your book,
But don't expect me to analyze or evaluate,
Like a schoolmaster at the end of term,
"His best subject is…" or "He needs coaching in…";
All that stuff. Indeed, why should I?
As you say yourself, *'John warns me of nostalgia*
And I suppose he's right—but what the hell—
What are poems for but for celebration
Of our time on earth, the years behind us
And ahead?' Oh yes, I've heard it said
that you write too much, and need to be selected:
That your style is derivative:
That you can be trite or sentimental:
Which may be all true. It doesn't matter.

You've put it down, as best you can, all of it—
And these aren't really poems at all, but parts
Of some huge epic which is your life,
lived as you know it, in the city of Toronto.
You feel the pressure, and record,
'Why does your loneliness surge up, why does that ugliness, despair,
Hit you between the eyes because you stand
On a bridge late at night, because you look down,
Down, at the dark, water, because your eyes move out into
               the darkness? Haven't you seen
The river before, don't you know it runs, smells like a sewer?
Haven't you choked on the smoke from these factories
Looking in the night like the tombs of many ghosts?'
Or mesmerized, fascinated by what appals you,
The Girl at the Corner of Elizabeth and Dundas,
'You want it or you don't
'You've got five bucks or no
I'm twenty-one I ain't

---

[1] Review of Raymound Souster *The Selected Poems* ed. Louis Dudek (Toronto: Contact Press 1956)

Got any time to waste
You want it or you don't
Make up your Jesus mind.'
Or bitter, thinking you've been had,
'After the usual routine questions
The doctor settled back in his chair,
"Knowing your mother's history
There was no need even to see you,
Your ailment was clearly foretold..."
When his bill came in the next week
I understood why only the rich
Can afford the luxury of migraine.'

Not unaware of another disease,
An occupational one for poets,
'Having written—or so he tells us—
At least one immortal poem,
He isn't content with this (the fool)
But has turned out another dozen.'

You've put your heart in it
And you've put it down straight—
Which is a heck of a lot more
Than most of us can boast.
You've been at it for over 15 years
And a habit like that isn't broken.
I hope I'm still around to read your ultimate
Unselected Collected Poems. Go to it.

Gael

Saint-Denys-Garneau

Hector de Saint-Denys Garneau (as his name was registered at birth) was born in Montreal in 1912, the son of a well-to-do banker, and never seems to have had any anxieties about money. His family had been in Quebec since at least 1655 when the marriage is recorded of Louis Garneau (who came from Poitou in France). His paternal grandfather was a poet: Alfred Garneau (1836–1904).

He spent some of his childhood at a rural *manoir* (dating from 1830) which had been associated with the family for several generations, about 25 miles north-west of Quebec city, and like most of that generation, his secondary and university education was largely supervised by the Jesuits. For some years he was at Art School in Montreal but gave up art for writing.

He published only one book of poems, *Regards et jeux dans l'espace* in 1937, after which he did continue to write but withdrew more and more into himself, and died in 1943, only thirty-one.

He had been taken ill in 1928, when he was only sixteen, with a serious heart problem (possibly rheumatic valvular disease, a common disability for young adults in that era) which is what eventually killed him, although he does not appear to have been a complete invalid, and in fact collapsed while alone on a canoe trip.

The awareness that he was marked for an early death, while still an adolescent, made a dramatic impression on the content of his writing. Robert Elie in his introduction to the 1949 edition of the poems, comments on some sort of religious crisis. "To his great astonishment, he discovered himself to be deeply Christian and yet had believed himself pagan, and the teachers of his youth had despaired of him achieving the certitudes of the average Catholic."

It must be remembered how profoundly Catholic Quebec was at that time. I recall meeting a young man in 1954 who told me that in the small rural towns where he had grown up, copies of a book like *Candide* passed furtively from hand to hand even if one could find a copy.

Elie, who had known him personally, also adds, enigmatically, that "he was not able to conceive of any love but 'charity'" (that is, religious or non-physical love) and there may have been an associated sexual crisis, not necessarily different to the experience of many adolescents.

I first encountered his poems in 1955 in the volume *Poésies complètes* (Montreal: Fides, 1949). This contains the poems of the one book published during his life, plus an equivalent group of posthumously collected poems, written subsequent to the 1937 collection and which are homogenous with the earlier poems in technique and preoccupations. This remains the essential "Saint-Denys-Garneau" (He signed his name in different ways but I have adopted this form since it is what he used for the 1937 book). Since then, a carefully edited and annotated *Oeuvres complètes* (with his name without the second hyphen) has been published (Université de Montréal, 1971). This gathers together his journals, correspondence, scattered items of prose, as well as a considerable body of juvenilia. This last is of interest to show the sort of poetic context in which he grew up, and the dramatic break he made with that past in the poems he wrote from 1935 onwards.

There is also a considerable body of comment, criticism and associated biographical material, as he is now considered one of the main progenitors of contemporary poetry in Quebec. Certainly his poems exerted a great influence on the young poets starting to write and publish in the late Forties and early Fifties, although as so often happens, the freshness of approach is probably not so apparent to readers today.

A volume of English translations of the *Poésies complètes* appeared in 1975 by John Glassco (Toronto: Oberon Press) with a good general introduction.

This account will ignore the themes and preoccupations of the poems, what they appear to describe and explore, which are essentially the dramas and often painful realisations of his inner life, even the paradoxes and absurdities. Instead, it will try to outline what first struck and interested me and which John Glassco has so aptly described as "the marvellous prosody which never failed him [and] may survive everything else (that is, the mental and emotional happenings which that prosody served to express, and all the later commentaries trying to unravel or paraphrase)".

Taking a stanza at random from toward the end of the posthumous poems, as it happens part way through a poem, Saint-Denys-Garneau writes:

Mon coeur cette pierre qui pèse en moi
Mon coeur pétrifié par ce stérile arrêt
Et regard retourné vers les feux de la ville
Et l'envie attardée aux cendres des regrets
Et les regrets perdus vers les pays possibles

(My heart this stone heavy [which weighs down] within me
My heart petrified [turned to stone]
by this sterile [fruitless] halt [stop]
And glance turned back toward the lights [fires] of the town
And yearning [desire] delayed [set back]
to the ashes of regrets [remorse]
And the regrets lost
toward possible [potential] countries [landscapes])

There is a characteristic and carefully orchestrated advance of the language in pace with the thought, as it were, step by step, stone by stone (frequent images in his work), precisely linked and progressive, where the abstractions become almost particulate objects and the particulate objects metaphors. The technique is not always as systematic or as closely worked as in this example, but is usually implicit or not far away.

Although I think that a great deal of Garneau's poetry, in terms of structure of language, does translate very well, compared with much French poetry, the problems here become obvious.

Les feux de la ville in the context of someone halting to look back, is the image of a town seen after dark, because *feux* is often used where in English we would use "lights". But there is also the resonance of "fires" which is needed to link with the "ashes" of the next line. But to translate "the fires of the town" or something equivalent introduces awkward associations in English, of houses on fire or outdoor bonfires. Unless of course, one is able to resonate with the image of Lot looking back on the destruction of Sodom, which is probably behind some of this, knowing Garneau's very religious education, but this is not immediately accessible to most modern readers. Even then the link "fire/ashes" is more immediate and still present in the French.

Similarly, there are the resonances between *regard* and *l'envie*, and the difficulty of translating the latter, which in French has a range of meaning from the casual "to fancy something" through to a deep "longing". It can be frivolous and tragic, and a certain lightness, even playfulness of tone amid the desperation of much of what is expressed, is characteristic of Garneau's best work. It is significant that the title of his 1937 book was *Regards et jeux dans l'espace*.

There is also the auditory prosody of the last line, all those "r"s and "p"s. And the further resonance, to passages in other poems of the *perdus* where the "lost" becomes almost a noun (substantive) with a particular physical presence of its own.

Although there are a number of his poems which are very effective in isolation as single poems (such as 'Cage d'oiseau' / 'Bird Cage', or the delightful 'C'en fut une de passage dans notre monde') and which inevitably are more accessible in a selection of translations, there is an overall cohesion and interdependence, evident in both the 1937 book and the enlarged posthumous *Poésies complètes*.

This is accentuated by the layout, which was apparently very carefully stipulated by Garneau, so that it can often be difficult to know which passages are separate poems, which are sections or parts of other poems. Many of the posthumously gathered poems have this same quality and appear to be fragments in that they occur in journals or on backs of scraps of paper. However, the word fragment is not necessarily useful and raises questions of definition, since a fragment, like a sketch in visual art, can sometimes be as complete and achieved as something more formally worked and presented. Or they could be categorised as sections of a larger composition, where the linkages with each other are thematic, reinforcing the effect of certain words and images by repetition and variation.

For example, on p.173 of the FIDES edition, there is the fragment (or should it be labelled the 'poem'?):

> Des navires bercés dans un port
> Doux bercements avec des souvenirs de voyage
> Puis on trouve seuls les souvenirs errants
> Qui reviennent et ne trouvent pas de port
> Souvenirs sans port d'attache
> Trouvent le port déserté
> Un grand lieu sans vaisseux

Ignoring the problems of translation here (*port d'attache* doesn't just mean "port of origin or registration" but also the port at the end of a journey), there is the characteristic building up of key words and images.

Then on the next page (another poem? a new fragment? a linked passage or even counterpoint?) there is introduction of *la mer*, and *un tournoiement d'oiseau* (and again there is a problem that this can be translated as "a swirl of birds" but that *un tournoiement* is also "a dizziness") and in subsequent lines the repetition, slightly varied in linkages of the previous *souvenirs* and *port d'attache*.

The last line of this passage is *Un tournoiement d'oiseaux sans port d'attache*, which further advances and unifies the imagery, with the further resonance of *souvenirs* (since, also earlier, *sans port d'attache*) and perhaps, if one were to attempt to translate into English, the metaphoric implication of "a dizziness of memories without place of origin or destination"?

British Poets

What Is Poetry *About*?

Some appreciations and digressions in regard to Tom Leonard's 'Radical Renfrew' [1]

[Note: It is assumed that the reader is familiar with the general outline of the book which consists of a comprehensive selection of poems "from the extensive archives of Paisley Central Library", nearly all of them by little known and locally published writers over the period of roughly 1750–1915, with the main focus on the later nineteenth century, plus a long statement by the editor. In the words on the back cover it "challenges the view of nineteenth-century West of Scotland literature which sees it as a desert in which a few 'minor figures' bloomed: it asserts that people have been deprived of a whole literature of what they once held to be valid poetry." The introduction closely argues why and how this has come about.]

The opening sentence of the introduction raises questions that appear to me to be more properly considered in a discussion of society. The paragraph then continues: "But poetry has been so defined in the public mind as usually to exclude the possibility of social conflicts appearing. The belief is widespread that poetry is not about the expression of opinion, not about politics, not about employment, not about what people actually do with their time between waking and falling asleep each day; not about what they eat, not about how much the food costs."

It is the use of the word *poetry* without further qualification that I would query. I find myself re-phrasing it, since the meaning appears to be implicit: "But *the subject matter* of poetry has been so defined…" and "The belief is widespread that *the subject matter* of poetry is not about…" and so on.

This meaning or emphasis of meaning in regard to what is meant by poetry is strongly reinforced by 'A Guide to the Location of Some Different Themes' listing the poems under Religion, Alcohol, Emigration, Employment etc., some categories subdivided such as those about Alcohol into "favourable", "alcoholism and domestic life", "temperance poems" etc. There are Anti-Ruling-Class, Feminist, even Astronomy and Microscopy poems.

The next paragraph begins "To an extent the connection between poetry and school has been the problem…" and goes on "…the trouble lies in the notion that poetry has to be *taught* in the first place, and that

---

[1] Tom Leonard (ed.) *Radical Renfrew: Poetry in the West of Scotland from the French Revolution to the First World War* (Edinburgh: Polygon 1990).

More Words

there is a professional caste of people best equipped so to do" and to give "guidance in a classroom as to how best ultimately to pass exams about it."

He goes on to trace this back to the early and mid 19th century invention of Literature as a subject in schools with the necessary corollary of a canon of works which embodied what was believed to be of cultural value, what was good for children and people to read, with the exclusion of what was not.

"Literature shrinks to Teachable Literature … Generation after generation has been *taught* that a poem itself has as it were to pass an exam before it can earn the right to be called a poem … [and] … only those people who have passed exams about poems, can give a new would-be poem the new exam necessary to decide whether it was a poem or not."

Again, in all this, appears to be the implicit identification that it is *the subject matter* which is what poetry is *about*, that literature is a matter of "social, moral and political values" and that this is, in the words of the Catechism, "the Chief End".

The disagreement is only in regard to the rigidity of that canon, its restriction, its close association with the exercise of power by particular groups in society, and not in regard to "the Chief End" which the writer appears to assume is the expression of opinions, ideas and values.

*

The bulk of the introduction then goes on, among other issues, to discuss this association and to point out to what considerable extent such a canon, mediated through mass education, has become a means of social and political control. There is a linkage with the use of language. Whether this is more peculiar to the British Isles than other parts of the world might be argued. Orwell spoke of the English being "branded on the tongue at birth" and it may be less so in Scotland but it is certainly a potent social force.

There are shrewd and pertinent remarks about elitist ideas as to what is acceptable as "Scots" and the relationship of that to how people actually speak, and the enormous pressure and influence of the educational system on how children are allowed to express themselves.

There are also some interesting distinctions between (1) *the* human being that we perceive ourselves to be at birth, unique and alone in the universe, and the sense of (2) *this* human being which we become, distinct and individual, unlike any other, and the importance of passing through the sense of (3) *a* human being, which many evade or escape, no more or less than any other, and without which we are likely to lack any sense of real identification, or equality with others.

*

All of this may read like an uneasy (or even glib?) effort to summarise what are obviously much more complex statements and arguments. Yet in trying to make explicit one reader's understanding of at least part of what Leonard expresses, it is to be hoped that this may be part of that dialogue which, in Leonard's words, may be "all that literature is." Certainly, it is an essential part.

If there are many issues which I have ignored, that is not intended as any judgement on their importance or otherwise but merely that there are areas into which I feel less confidence or have less incentive to venture; and he ranges widely!

But on the points concerning "the Chief End" of poetry and that of the canon of literature, Leonard's introduction brings refreshment and challenge on what seem to me fundamental concerns.

*

Two personal experiences, in regard to the second of these concerns.

Some years ago I was talking with a friend whom I had come to know because of admiration for poems he had written. He then happened to be earning his living teaching English Literature at a University and had just finished conducting some end-of-year *vivas*. He told me of a student who had expressed the opinion that there was more "value" (I forget exactly how expressed) in the poems of Edith Sitwell than in those of T.S. Eliot. He had marked the student down and expressed satisfaction in doing this, even that it was a blow for all that was important in literature. This was not on the basis of the quality of the comment on the poems, but because no one could be allowed to pass who did not value Eliot above Edith Sitwell. This was not, it should be noted, in respect of any particular single poem of either of them.

I was astonished into silence. Looking back, I realise that although I had accepted the idea, rightly or wrongly, that at primary and even secondary school level, some didactic teaching of the nature of "these are examples of what poetry is about" was necessary, at university level I had assumed freedom of thought, even that it was encouraged.

I am not asserting that all teaching is of this sort, and it was some years ago, but what contact I have had with teaching at a university level has not encouraged me that things are vastly different, for better or for worse, according to your choice.

The other experience has been more recent. I was approached by a well established but not large-circulation magazine, asking for a contribution within specified limits on 'The State of Poetry'. Quotations were appended from various poets, mostly contemporary and by no means all published by Faber & Faber.

After some thought and inability to generalise on the extraordinary volume and variety of poems being currently written and published and even read, I decided to take the words at their other primary meaning as "The State", through its various powerful agencies: the Educational System, the Universities, the various Arts Councils, the British Council, even in its now perhaps diminishing role, the BBC.

I wrote on the theme of "who pays the piper plays the tune" and questioned whether the State had ever before so powerfully subsidised and controlled the production and publication of poetry, and wondered "to what end?"

Perhaps needless to say, my contribution was not printed. In fact, I did not even get it returned or the courtesy of a note to explain why. Was it that it was not sufficiently well written? That judgement I could accept. That it was not relevant? That might be argued, but was fair opinion. Or did they exclude it simply because they disagreed?

*

To what end? The selection of the poems included in the anthology appears to be based on the assumption that a poem is anything written in a recurrent metrical form, usually but not always with a pattern of end rhymes. Whether this can be distinguished from verse or whether such a distinction is possible or desirable, is not mentioned.

I am not arguing here that there should or should not be such a distinction, but merely pointing out the obvious: that there is an implicit identification of verse with poetry without any explicit statement to that effect.

Many of the examples are the texts of words which were intended to be sung, and the tunes to which the words were composed are frequently recorded, but there is nothing to indicate whether there is anything distinctive about a song, or not.

This is curious, since as an art form, songs have always had a much greater provenance and wider subject matter, as a natural vehicle for expression by ordinary people (as opposed to the written literature of an elite) and perhaps with a much longer history. The oral use of verse (that is, a stylised and rhythmical use of language) never written down at all or only much later, chanted in a formal way, is usually closely related to song.

Both of these means of expression may have also been part of the codified literature of an intellectual elite or the State (the Homeric works and *Beowulf* are obvious examples) but I think a case can be made for the generalisation that in song, often anonymously propagated and handed down, there was (and even still is) a very vigorous and persistent art-form which expresses cultural and artistic values in regard to verse or poetry and in spite of whatever literary canon a ruling elite might try to dictate.

*

The nearest to any discussion of what might be specific to poetry as a vehicle for writing as distinguished from prose or any other form, comes in the comment on James Thomson's *City of Dreadful Night*. There are interesting suggestions as to how it may be read as something not totally introspective but even as an objective depiction of aspects of the industrial city, the experience of which would have been almost unknown before Thomson's birth.

There is also a discussion of an orchestrated structure to the work, even mention of Bruckner's music, chiefly in regard to the cultural implications of being free or not to enjoy such music, and by implication, such orchestration in a poem.

Leonard does state at one point: "It's not the place here to start a technical analysis of the poem". This at least opens up the possibility that poetry (in the sense of some quality that makes us designate a particular assemblage of words as a poem) might indeed have something to do with technique, a use of language; and that the subject matter or opinions expressed in a poem, are not necessarily all that is important, or even primary.

One may, of course, make the choice that it is. But in that case, surely the choice needs to be made explicit?

*

The poems in the anthology are of great variety, not just in subject matter but in technique, and specific comment is inevitably arbitrary. Some flow with the pace and vigour of good songs. Some, although labelled as songs, don't read very easily to my ear (although admittedly the tune, unidentified here, may help) such as the anonymous verses, 'The Hour of Retribution's Nigh' the first verse of which ends,

> Fit cradle, tyrant power to nurse!
> Soft couch of sloth, where despots lie!
> Legitimacy, freemen's curse.
> The hour of retribution's nigh!

Marion Bernstein's writing is a good example of a problem which I feel exists, though others may disagree. She is represented by seven pieces, and was known and respected by her contemporaries. She wrote a reply to one of Jessie Russell's poems, who wrote again in further reply.

In terms of ideas and themes she has one of the most striking groups of poems (or verses, according to your choice) with an outspoken "feminism" all the more remarkable for its clarity in the context of her time (circa 1875) and circumstances (she was a partly crippled music teacher) and sardonic, sometimes even self-mocking humour.

Quotation is necessarily selective. On first reading, her verses appeared to me often awkward, even plodding, occasionally just careless or perfunctory.

> Pray, in what way is wrong redressed,
>   But by conceding right?
> And Woman Suffrage is the best
>   For which our sex can fight.
>
> You speak of women's wages
>   Being scandalously small;
> Believe me, Woman Suffrage
>   Soon would find a cure for all.

There is the irony of 'Manly Sports':

> A cheer for fox-hunting! Come all who can dare
>   Track this dangerous animal down to its lair;
> 'Tis first trapped, then set free for the huntsmen to follow
>   With horses and hounds, and with heart-stirring halloo!

The "halloo" rhyme is characteristic. There is a poem entitled 'A Dream' which is a fantasy of improbabilities, however much to be desired and which ends:

> All the churches attended a conference
>   At which every sect agreed
> That an erring opinion was not so bad
>   As a false word or wicked deed.
>
> At this I felt sure there was some mistake,
>   It seemed such a *strange* idea!
> My eyes opened wide, and that made me wake,
>   Now wasn't the vision queer?

I find it difficult to read this as other than clumsy or impatient writing, yet in places she achieves effects of unexpected intensity, as in 'Human Rights' (the entire poem):

Man holds so exquisitively tight
To everything he deems his right;
If woman wants a share, to fight
She has, and strive with all her might.

But we are nothing like so jealous
As any of you surly fellows;
Give us our rights and we'll not care
To cheat our brothers of their share.

Above such selfish *man-like* fright,
We'd give fair play, let come what might,
To he or she folk, black or white,
And haste the reign of Human right.

By contrast, there are the verses of the Reverend John Macleod. The rhythms flow smoothly, the rhymes are impeccable, the diction poetic and unexceptionable within the conventions of the time, as in 'Passing Morven', written perhaps 20 years later, which begins:

Down Mull's dark sound from port to port
  The vessel holds upon her way,
From green Loch Aline's wooded shore
  To yonder castle-crowned bay.

And silent 'mid a motley throng
  Of strangers—on her deck I stand
Watching with thoughts unutterable
  The glory of the gliding sand.

O land of Morven! dearer far
  To me than fairest spot of earth;
O land on which my eyes first looked,
  The land that gave my fathers birth.

This is not intended to make any absolute judgement between John Macleod and Marion Bernstein but to illustrate what appears to me to be a problem which this book raises by implication.

There are of course gross differences in subject matter between Macleod and Bernstein, as there are of gender and social class but

Jessie Russell wrote on very similar subjects to Marion Bernstein and was of a broadly similar background. Her poems are technically more conventionally accomplished. She even uses Scots when it suits her purpose, and skilfully. Two verses from 'Signs of our Times' (dated to 1875):

> 'The labourer's worthy o'his hire,'
>   But where's the body willing
> Tae draigle through the daily mire
>   When a' the hire's a shilling.
>
> Faix, no! he'd rather starve belyve;
>   But, hark! the clapper's clanging,
> The only trade that seems tae thrive
>   Is 'gentlemanly' hanging.

They make an interesting comparison, and Bernstein's rougher, one might even say cruder touch is often, to my ear, more effective. This is not a plea for naive technique, but to try to extend the discussion as to what is of interest in the poems and what we might value. There are orthodoxies as to what makes for good writing and questions of what is considered permissible, beyond simply those of the opinions expressed, or the subjects chosen.

To take another example, with two anti-alcohol poems, both overtly saying the same thing, yet with a difference. Daniel King and Robert Semple were born within three years of each other. Semple's poem begins:

> When day is past and work is o'er,
>   And night comes on the scene,
> We gladly hail, ere morning comes,
>   The hours that intervene;
> But when the day comes to its close,
>   And Sunday comes in sight,
> How sweet to spend with loving hearts
>   A sober Saturday night!

Competent, but not very stirring? King's verses begin:

More Words

> Yer fou', oh, Robin Duff, yer fou',
>   Ye haena got a fit to stan',
> The smell that's comin' frae yer mou'
>   Wad sicken ony sober man;
> An' yet ye'll tell me to my cheek
>   'Twas harmless a' the drink ye got;
> Preserve us, Rab, ye canna speak,
>   Ye leein', dirty, drucken sot.

Even ignoring the smeddum of fun in the latter, surely a more effective way of saying what it sets out to say? This is not to deny the interest of including Semple's poem in the overall scope of the collection but to illustrate that the variety of the book is not just in the subject matter, as the presentation might suggest.

Nor, I would suggest, is it simply a matter of English versus Scots, of educated versus natural, of literary versus spoken. If Semple uses "received English", King is not far from "received Burns". One can use either of them effectively, or not. There is a vigour to Marion Bernstein's "received English" as there is affectation to some of the "received Burns".

But, in general, there is indeed more ease of expression, and vitality to those poems in the anthology which are written in Scots, for all that it carries the risk of being pawky or quaint. It is probably closer, so far as one can tell, to the actual speech of those writing in it, and usually moves with a less stilted pace.

Whether Semple's poem was closer to how he actually spoke than King's, to how he spoke, or the other way around, it is of course, impossible to guess. Tom Leonard has a lot of great interest to say about "A literature in which it is possible for a writer to be nobody else but his or her self…" and he well may be right that the barrier to this is in the social/political structure of society, especially as expressed in education.

He contrasts Community Art with High Art; and it is possible that questions such as "Is this well written?" or "Is it a poem at all?" are a luxury that only High Art can afford, are perhaps even a characteristic feature of such an art.

Does this then mean that any piece of verse, any writing, regardless of considerations of skill is valid as Community Art? Perhaps in order to assert the importance of "to be nobody else but his or her self…", such an approach to Art may be necessary, at least in the short-term. But in the longer term?

In other words, what is poetry *about*? Is it merely to provide a means for expression of the self, for the expression of opinions and ideas? Such a need is manifestly needed and the terms and conventions of what may or may not be expressed, and how, must not be constrained by an educational system, controlled by an elite, through the state, or by economic power. But if that is all that poetry is, just one more means of expression, and to be valued in terms of what it expresses, then it would seem to me to deny, or at least denigrate, anything distinctive for poetry as a means (as distinct from other means) and make it in the end *about* nothing. And Leonard manifestly cares too much about poetry, for that.

*

The last sentence of the opening paragraph of the Introduction begins "[The belief is widespread that poetry]… is not in the voice of ordinary discourse…" There are also extensive comments later in regard to the problems of language in terms of specific diction; and particularly in regard to spoken Scots as opposed to that language (in which I write this) variously called Received English, Queen's English, whatever; and which the educational system, one of Leonard's chief targets, perpetuates. It is perhaps the nearest he comes to the possibility that poetry might be (or at least, might also be) an art form that uses language as its material.

On page xxxi he remarks, and it needs to be said far more often than it is, "But no caste has the right to possess, or even imagine it has the right to possess, bills of exchange on the dialogue between one human being and another." He then goes on, "And such dialogue is all that Literature is."

What I would wish to query (and I don't think it gets queried often enough) is that "all". Although this piece, one might hope, is also part of that dialogue.

Identity and Ideology or What Happened to the Poem

Readers of this from outwith Scotland may find some of the detail unfamiliar or irrelevant but the preoccupation with a quest for "a distinctive Scottish psyche" must be familiar even in countries not so obviously culturally beleaguered. Similarly, the assumption that poems have no value except in the service of particular ideologies—political, intellectual, linguistic, even religious—or must have social usefulness, is international, and not just within an academic context.

The Faber Book of 20th Century Scottish Poetry, edited by Douglas Dunn (1992), is one of the most prominent of recent anthologies of Scottish poetry. Readers may agree or disagree with the choice of poems, even of poets, and there will always be omissions in such selections that any reader may regret, and inclusions that can be questioned. But the editor is not only a highly acclaimed poet but also a professor of poetry at one of Scotland's most prestigious universities and although it is only the poems themselves that finally matter, his ideas and comments on his choices, in the lengthy introduction, may fairly attract comment.

Where he starts is significant, a quotation from a book review by T.S. Eliot in 1919, entitled: 'Was There a Scottish Literature?' Dunn comments on a contemporary book surveying Scottish Literature and quotes Eliot's assessment in regard to this, that although there may have been such a definable literature in the past that "…there is no longer any tenable distinction to be drawn for the present day between [English and Scottish] literatures."

Later in the introduction he quotes again from Eliot's review "The basis for one literature is one language", and thus, while arguing that Eliot in his review had misjudged the situation, and depreciating Eliot's "crudely potted history and questionable philology", the general approach and categories which Eliot employs are assumed to be valid.

MacDiarmid is then introduced in rebuttal—although to be fair to Eliot, it was only four years earlier that MacDiarmid's poems had been published—and it is suggested that MacDiarmid, by inventing (or re-inventing) a national language, thus defines a national literature. What is immediately noticeable is that the argument is that it is not that MacDiarmid's poems are of a quality as poetry which obviates Eliot's analysis, but that it is MacDiarmid's ideology, that *this* was "…

the heart of MacDiarmid's struggle... nothing less than the recovery of a distinctive Scottish psyche, and its true objectives and concerns, from the slow sundering initiated by the Union..."

Attention is then briefly focussed on the three crucial books of 1925/1926, noting very aptly that their poetry "...remained undamaged by the extensive prose suburbs that grew up around ... The same cannot be said of his later poetry." However, what is signalled as of value is not the freshness of diction, the particularity and the music, but that the poetry is "...a gesture through which the reader witnesses a lapsed language modifying itself in order to engage with a new aesthetic."

Finally the commentary focuses on a particular poem from that period: 'The Eemis Stane', noting that it is structured on a single "daring, speculative image". But further specific analysis is then abandoned in favour of "The poem seems to withhold its meaning... It is the poem's mysteriousness that is exact, not its meaning. It is a poem that persists in a state of permanent unfamiliarity."

Following this there are three pages of ideological and abstract speculation in relation to MacDiarmid's era, and the various thought systems current, ranging through Ouspensky, Kierkegaard, etc. etc., even including a nod to Williams' *In the American Grain*. He pertinently notes that since for Williams the fact of "an American nation" could be taken for granted, for MacDiarmid, "The difference is that MacDiarmid was trying to make a nation as well as poetry".

However, curiously, other than Ouspensky, there is no mention of those Russian writers and philosophers, especially Solovyov, with whose writings MacDiarmid was closely engaged.

It is a fascinating analysis, as it undoubtedly was to MacDiarmid for whom it dissipated a lot of energy as well as helping to generate it, but the reader may wonder what relevance it has to the value of the poems as poems.

Then, suddenly, with relief, we are back to a specific poem, the justly remarkable 'Water Music', and there is generous acknowledgment of some of its qualities, the "love of the language it uses, a devotion to its exuberance and peculiarity... [its] lexical splendours... revels... rhapsody..." There is even, finally, a quotation of four specific lines of poetry, which is identified as the opening stanza of the poem.

This stanza is predicated on a reference to "Joyce" and "Anna Livvy" and one can almost hear the sigh of relief as the commentary is then able to digress into MacDiarmid's interest in Joyce, and other related aspects of the modernist Twenties. But these four lines, which are quoted with such enthusiasm, are *not* the opening stanza of the poem. They are an epigraph, printed in italics, and repeated again at the end; and a way of framing the poem, making a dedication of homage, and perhaps indulging one of MacDiarmid's particular hobby-horses. Fair enough. But that the editor of this anthology chooses to pass them off as part of the poem, chooses to focus his comment on them instead of on the poem, is expressive of where his true interest appears to lie.

The general survey of poetry written by others than MacDiarmid has the inevitable problem of coping with very diverse individuals, often writing with different objectives and assumptions as to what poetry is intended to accomplish. This is a genuine problem and there is often recognition of it, while at the same time, a wish to make a tidy and intellectually structured pattern of the whole. Frequently the strain of this shows.

He obviously recognises and indeed appreciates considerable qualities in the poems of Norman MacCaig. Might some of MacCaig's poems actually be more accomplished, more worth spending time reading, than some of MacDiarmid's? This possibility lurks behind the oddity of the commentary, that he can't acknowledge achievement while at the same time can't always dismiss it, and one gets passages such as this, about MacCaig's work: "As a body of poetry made up for the most part of short lyrics, brief discursive narratives and satires, it can seem to resist identification as the work of a major writer. However, what finally makes it as such is the importance of its themes, and the extent to which poem after poem seeks to define and clarify the individual's relationship to the world."

In other words, some sort of ideological usefulness has to be found, some intellectual or sociological relevance, or the poems cannot be allowed to be "important".

There are parallel difficulties with Edwin Morgan's poems, which celebrate diversity and invention, the unexpected and the bizarre, and are technically restless, reluctant to repeat or fall into any perfunctory pattern. Nor is there any easily labelled ideology. For some reason

Morgan's relationship to the wider international modern "avant-garde" (and not just poetry written in all the various derivatives and evolutions of Anglo-Saxon) is not acknowledged, perhaps because of the effort to fit everything into "the recovery of a distinctive Scottish psyche". Instead we get comment such as: "Openness to change, humour and liveliness have made his work attractive to younger readers in Glasgow… His urban *joie de vivre* provides a balance to MacCaig's predilection for more rural and natural settings…" Morgan's evident linguistic interests are not related to those of MacDiarmid, perhaps because not fitting easily into the values that have been postulated, and clearly extending beyond Scotland.

The final paragraph of the commentary picks up again on the historical categories propounded by Eliot for "Scottish literature", while amending them for recent times, and ends with: "It has been a hectic century for Scottish poetry, one filled with thrilling turbulence, and in which the stakes have been high—the survival of a national identity."

The survival of a national identity is certainly not to be scorned and striking poems have been written in response to the struggle for it, but one might think that the achievement of a body of poems of which we might be proud was an objective more appropriate. Or are poems merely incidental to whatever intellectual framework is constructed to frame or justify them?

(Signed)
Thomas Lundin[1]

---

[1] Thomas Lundin was an occasional pseudonym used by the author. Lundin was Gael Turnbull's middle name.

Resonances & Speculations, upon Reading Roy Fisher's *City*

Fisher writes of his city: "The sensitive, the tasteful, the fashionable, the intolerant and powerful, have not moved through it as they have moved through London, evaluating it, altering it deliberately, setting in motion wars of feeling about it. Most of it has never been seen."[1]

> Only a landscape that I find
> [...]
> Whenever I cast back my mind—
> The chequered shadows and the angled lines
> Of puckered streets and beetle roofs
> In a brick-infested town
> Where only the damp cobbles shine...[2]

Yes, there it is: to see it. Has anyone seen it?

Another city: Tyneside. I remember the allotments, the cabbages and cauliflowers in ranks and rows. Beyond, a cemetery: the headstones arranged. And nearer, the row houses, row after row after row of them, with the gates spaced equally, each with its matchbox garden.

In the alleys, cobblestones—one, two, three ... and forever.

A few collieries, in bits of faded green field outside. Great standing constructions with spilled earth, wheels, smoke, their energy absorbed, secreted, intently working far underground.

Churches scattered here and there among the houses. Stiff non-conformist fronts. Cheap coloured glass windows, thick with coal grime. Purple bricks set in patterns, for ornament.

Always a moisture on the stone and on the red brick walls and shining on the cobblestones. At night, reflecting the light that came from the street lamps. In bed in an upstairs room, to look out of a window between partly drawn curtains. The drops upon the glass, alive with refracted light. Or to listen there in the dark to the distant shunting engines: chug chug, rattle, rebound, clank clank, choof choof.

---

[1] from Roy Fisher, 'The Sun Hacks' in *City*, reprinted in *The Long and the Short of It. Poems 1955–2005* (Tarset: Bloodaxe Books 2005).

[2] from Gael Turnbull 'A Landscape and a Kind of Man' first published in *Trio* (1954), and reprinted in *There are words... Collected Poems* (Exeter: Shearsman Books 2006).

Or walking: how many streets to walk! My feet on the pavement, with the cracks between the paving stones and the neatly set curb and a gutter with sweet wrappers and bits of soaked newspaper. A drain at intervals. I would peer down between the bars of the grating, full of fear at the thought of the depth and that I might fall in. How could I get out? Or if I should drop something down. How could I possibly get it back? The irrevocable darkness below into which something or someone might fall.

I would walk all afternoon, past small grocer shops and tobacconists, the occasional cobbler or butcher. Pubs also, with curiosity and fear: a smell of malt and hops, of potency, of heavy men breathing heavily and speaking heavily. As I walked aimlessly, endlessly it would seem, until I would lose myself, but never really lost. Always to come out on some recognizable landmark, a railway line or a tramline, or the high boarded sides of a shut shipyard or factory. To turn me back again, to retrace myself. Until the restlessness was assuaged by weariness. My head full of northern monsters, of the Sagas and early Saxon kings. My face touched by cold winds coming inland from the sea; that sea which I rarely saw but always knew.

*

Jarrow. Bede's chair. The old man with his histories and his students and his Faith. Now to stand in front of that queer little chair with its broad and yet narrow seat, and high back. Uncomfortable. Is it his chair? Why, if it is? Who would think to keep such a thing?

Or the building itself, the old monastery church with the little Saxon arches over the narrow windows: black stone, black with grime, blacker even than any of the houses. A deposit of years. Standing by itself, in an open place, almost in the country, a little apart. Of piled stones, of cut stones.

But bricks? A brick isn't a stone. Though cold as stone, and hard, and piled up, bit by bit, one by one.

Cement and concrete. Containing stone, derived from stone. All done with hands; and with flame to fire the brick and to calcine the limestone into lime—then slaked with water, to set, to become in turn impervious to water. To be impervious.

More Words

The last time I was on Tyneside, I had in my notebook an address which I had obtained, quite by chance, in Canada. It was given to me as the address of a certain writer, a poet, whose work I greatly admire. A scribbled address, in an adjacent town—a street and a number—to which I went one day, on an impulse.

It was a place I had known as a person. This was a man I had known only through his writing. But the conjunction happened, as it sometimes happens; as, at some time and some place, it must happen.

Up a slanting street, with a view out over the valley of the Tyne. Up some high steps, to an ordinary door, any door. With a man to open the door, to say, "Yes, I am —," and to greet me. A little amused perhaps at my obvious surprise that he existed. How could it be? And how could it be otherwise?

My first bizarre reaction: how much he was my story-book image of a scout-master, Then, another image, of dignity and humour. Later, in conversation, he said of someone else, "There was no side to him." The slightly old fashioned implication of *side*; and its enormously appropriate relevance.

We sat in the kitchen and talked. He spoke of his life and of the writing of poetry. Of the war and of his travels. Of Persia and Isfahan, of the wines of California, and of Los Angeles before the freeways came. Many places, many people.

He showed me a Koran, and translations from the Arabic, ornate and sinuous verse. Reading to me with a slight Northumberland accent, a roughness to the consonants.

[…]

If Wordsworth and Constable helped to establish a certain "landscape" in the last century, a work such as *City* is an effort to establish another landscape. Reading it, I am aware most immediately and obviously of its relationship to the *Paterson* of William Carlos Williams. If Fisher frequently comes to the same material as Williams, it is never from the same starting point or with the same intention. Williams in America is very eagerly concerned to find a myth, a vision, a means etc., which will give relevance to his city, which will provide him and his poetry with some sort of form through which and by which the man and the city and the poetry can have a community. Thus, for all the formlessness, in one sense, of *Paterson,* it is very deliberately willed. It is a work of great determination. If there is no form available then Williams, by sheer intent, will *will* such a form into existence.

And so we have the mind of a man being a kind of city, and a city being also, at times, a man; and the waterfall, and the run to the sea, and the other given signposts. Which relate to the work with difficulty, so that one feels that this declared structure is very much imposed upon the material out of an almost desperate necessity. The material thus escapes, overflows, almost contradicts the declared structure; and for all the focus upon *Paterson*, the city itself as a physical presence continually recedes from the reader. The attention is not so much upon what is actually there as it is upon how it may be useful to the commitment of the poem.

Fisher in the Midlands starts with no such overall concept. Rather he is concerned to perceive and to declare his perception; and that perception must find its own resting place. He looks out into his back garden. "It is a December afternoon, and it is raining. Not far from the window is a black marble statue of a long-haired, long-bearded old man... It is clearly not in its proper place; resting as it does across the moss of the raised border, it is appreciably tilted forward and to one side, almost as if it had been abandoned as too heavy by those who were trying to move it—either in or out."

Is it possible to know what one is doing while one is doing it? Possible, indeed, before the act, to have a certain intention. And possible, afterwards, to perceive what it is that one *has* done. But while one is involved? Surely in the happening of an action, all that can be willed is to give oneself as fully as possible to what is going on, to try above all to be true to the closest instinct of the moment, at each moment. Even when its pattern or its meaning may appear utterly lost. Then, later, from another vantage point, we may see what has happened.

And so, in writing, it is not a matter of a certain material which is *there,* as a fixed thing, upon which the writing feeds and works. The act of writing also serves to nourish the material. When we speak of something, we affect it. It isn't quite the same. As we cannot altogether *will* what we would say. The very language we use is not *mine* but is only *ours*; and what we would say, of any material, is shaped by those others both past and present; as it is also shaped by the meanings which are in the material itself, meanings which perhaps we discover rather than create.

If a landscape of a city is not a natural one, the landscape of a Constable is not a natural one either. What Constable depicted is the product of human hands and human will: equally so, a city. A natural landscape is almost a contradiction. What someone like Wordsworth took for nature was often the result of many thousands of years of human presence. Even when the peaks themselves had been hardly affected by human action, they were viewed from valleys which were rich with human presence, and which gave a setting and a relevance for the noble prospect.

I did not understand this until I had lived for some years in parts of northern Canada and the Western United States. There, in places, it is still possible to feel the natural world as a Turner or a Ruskin could never have done. A northern forest, lakes, rocks, muskeg, jackpine and spruce, hundreds of miles, without vantage point or relevance. It is like looking at an empty sheet of paper. In this sense, I would assert, the Alps and an industrial city in New Jersey are both landscape; but parts of the Sierras and the north of Canada, and so on, are as yet unwritten—that is to say, scarcely exist.

A friend wrote to me recently about the South Wales Bypass which he had seen in process of being built. A great furrow cut across the countryside, ignoring the existing villages, hedges and roads, to expose the dark earth beneath. It was as if, for the first time, there revealed, he had seen the earth, the ground. And it was as if looking into an emptiness. What he had supposed held and nourished the landscape was nothing at all. Nothing there, in one sense, under his feet on which he could stand—other than what was made or what he could make.

*

My impatience with the imagination arises from the fact that it won't serve my needs, that is, as a servant. Nor am I able to follow its sure precept, as I would a master. Rather, it is a reprieve under which, for a little time, I am able to see what lies in front of my nose. It is not a means to great exertion, but just a gift of the obvious.

*

I don't mean to pay a disproportionate attention to what might be mistaken for *bons mots* in Fisher's writing. They are not really a matter of the appropriate expression for the specific idea or image. They often have a gratuitous quality, and it is almost as if these expressions themselves were part with the physical presence of the city—as much "given" as any other detail.

Yet they give a personal colour to the writing, and tick in my mind afterwards. "…to feel vertically, like a blind wall, or thickly, like the tyres of a bus." "…a cemetery of performance." "…a twilight of aluminium." "…the night slides like a thaw" "winds of indigo" "cars …that sweat mercury and lead." To paraphrase another Fisher poem, not included here, I have the sensation of having truly wandered into somebody else's imagination. It isn't me. There is a puzzlement, even as the *rightness* seems obvious.

Not far from where I now live, there is a construction. I have occasion to pass it frequently, at all hours of the day and night. The situation is unusual: on the coast, within less than a hundred yards of the sea, surrounded by sand dunes, and with no other significant building for several miles about.

It is a large construction, of the height of at least three or four ordinary houses, roughly cubical in shape, with a chimney to one side. The chimney is slightly taller than the main mass of the building. The exterior is covered with a tangle of vertical and horizontal pipes of various sizes which presumably communicate with each other and with the centre. A few subsidiary sheds grouped at the base and a fence around complete the design.

It is visible, because of its size and because of its isolation, from a great distance in all directions. At night, it is lit by a profusion of small lights of an undistinguished faintly yellow tint, as well as a blinking red light on top of the chimney.

More Words

It is only as I write this, in a few spare moments of an overcast afternoon, that I realise that I cannot recall ever having seen a man there. Nor am I aware of where the access road connects with the main read. Yet, for all this, I have no doubt that there is an access road; and that the construction was made by men. As I have no doubt that it is used by men.

Some Notes on *The Ship's Orchestra* by Roy Fisher[1]

What can be done with it: this thing of being an artist? To bring something out of nothing? Absurd. Or to shape natural things, to order them, so as to give pleasure? But joy can't be shaped or ordered. Then is it some sort of practical joke? Laughable? And truly, desperately nothing to be laughed at.

*

Why the ship? But what else would serve? What more splendid means of doing what the snail does: who moves and yet never leaves home. Never has to go away.

On the ship, within the ship, a contained place, defined, in one sense quite static. Once set to sea, nothing can come aboard. Nothing can threaten from without. As equally, of course, one can't leave.

And the ocean, the movement upon it. One mile is like the next mile. The water parts in front and closes behind. No land marks. To go forward, yet leave nothing.

Something fearful in that, too. As if to leave everything behind. And yet, how can one be sure that the ship *does* move? Perhaps it doesn't. Perhaps it has run aground, and only the water flows past?

*

For an artist, what must concern him most closely is the means by which he practises his art. (Both accuracy and irony in that "practises"). Thus, for the musician, his instrument. But a dependence, an obligation in that. For it compels work, is a task-master, exerts bondage. Which is shameful.

Then the only hope (since the means itself can offer no escape) is to destroy that means. "…utter disposal of the instruments…" Only one problem: if his instrument exerts the greatest tyranny, it is also the object which is most dearly loved. Perhaps the only thing which is loved at all. The musician winces, to strike. Feels the pain of the blow, as against himself.

---

[1] Published by Fulcrum Press, London, in 1966. Reprinted in Roy Fisher *The Long and the Short of It. Poems 1955-2005* (Tarset: Bloodaxe Books 2005).

So, before the final disposal, the instrument must be given protection. "...white foam-rubber containers..." These set in further cylindrical containers. Elaborate identification of the cylinders. Further "...a continuous white tube into which the cylinders fit and in which they are moved pneumatically..."

But no ordinary place would be adequate for such a ceremony. A special place must be imagined. "...a hangar stretching some miles in all directions..." Further details of how it is painted, lighted. And so on. Until the instrument itself seems almost forgotten.

Thus two apparently irreconcilable, and yet equally desired things are accomplished. The object most feared and hated has become imprisoned in its wrappings, in its barracks edifice, in its prison. As the object most loved, most precious has been entombed, and is finally safe from harm, enshrined in its temple.

*

"The ship's orchestra is at sea!" At sea! I should think so. But open any page at random. Even sly. "Inside the sack, in here with me, I think." And peep out. When the coast seems clear. Sneak out. "She knows I have come out but she doesn't know where I am." Creep up behind her, Boo! "Between Amy's breasts by caterpillar tractor. And back again." Deliberate. Careful.

*

"Suppose she wears night dresses like the heavy shining pink one always, not just when I visit. That would be no joke". No. But what do we mean, then, by a joke? Indeed, jokes, the real ones, aren't funny. Though possibly nothing else to do but laugh. If one can, if one is merely a spectator.

And if we laugh, who are we laughing at? Or at what? The joke on us? Which is the best joke of all. And no joke. For the orchestra does not play. As an orchestra, "All the same, we're about to agree." The members of the orchestra? "And still the orchestra is about to agree." And what of the audience? "The question of our not being asked to play..." It is no longer even a question. Or if it was a question, what sort of question? No question of "will you play?" or of "won't you play?" but the question of "not being asked." Which is no question.

Though singly, to themselves, they play. Parts of an orchestra. "Amy has begun ... Long notes, staccato series. Methodical, clear, accurate ... a killer ... She must be feeling low to have to play." To have to! The necessity, the ignominy of it.

*

I must admit, to date, I haven't been able to read through *The Ship's Orchestra* from start to finish. In fact, I have difficulty reading more than a page or two at a time. Have difficulty reading more than a paragraph or two at a time. Have difficulty reading. Halted. Obstructed. Parody of *The Ship's Orchestra*, even writing this. Involved in an effort to reject the obstruction. Of not being able to make the effort to reject the obstruction. Involvement without acceptance. An aspect of the fascination of the book. Of its achievement. The inability to totally dispose of it. Arresting. Anti-cathartic.

And at the same time, infinitely diverting. One of the most truly comic books I have ever read. Or tried to read. With the happy anticipation that I may never finish it.

Edinburgh, May 1963

[Note: In May 1963 I came on a two (or three) week visit from California, travelling by way of Reykjavik (Icelandic Airlines) to Prestwick. Writing now, in 1996, I remember visiting my aunt in Uddingston, then coming by bus to Edinburgh. From here I went south by train but can only remember visiting Bill (W. Price) Turner in Leeds (he had gone there as Gregory Fellow, from Glasgow) and Michael Shayer in Worcester, though may have visited other friends. I then returned to Prestwick by way of Edinburgh.

This account was written at the time or very shortly after, and transcribing it, I have only cut a few redundant phrases and one personal reference, as well as clarifying some minor points. I was then 35 and even at the time was conscious that I wanted to record something out of the ordinary, as if living something that was already myth, and may well have sent the top copy to a friend or done it for my wife. There are details as if explaining something specifically for someone else, or as if writing a letter.

Ian had written to me shortly before hoping that I could get an Art book for him which wasn't available in Britain, and which I brought with me. I hadn't told him I was coming.]

24 Fettes Row. Last house in a row of Victorian buildings. Up two flights of broad stone stairs, well worn. Dark, damp, like a mine shaft. A little slip of paper on the door: Wild Hawthorn Press. Poor. Old. Tired. Horse.[1]

I ring. The door opens into a dark lobby, like a cave. For a moment it is as if the door had opened itself. Then a head appears around the edge and a thin body. I say "Mr. Finlay?" He says "Yes." I hold out the Dada book he had asked for, saying that he had ordered it and that I thought I had better make sure it got to him personally.

He peers at me, almost suspicious. I repeat myself and he still looks doubtful, touching the book with a long finger, looking at me as if I were joking.

Then I say "I'm Gael Turnbull" and he cries "Gael!" and his arms are out and we hug each other awkwardly. He calls to Jessie "Gael's here!" and to me "Coom in, coom in!" We go through the hall into a back room. The sun is streaming in through a partly open window. Almost dazzles me after the dark.

---

[1] Respectively, the names of Finlay's small press and his magazine.

A big table covered with books and papers. Stacks of Wild Hawthorn books and POTHs on the floor. A brass frame bed at one side. Pictures and drawings and lists of names and addresses pinned to the wall. A gas fire lit, it still being a bit cold so early. We stare at each other in amusement, as if it were all a huge joke, as it is.

Ian thinner than me and a bit more stooped, his head seeming too big for his body, his eyes too big for his head, with a big nose and small chin. Rather sharp, curved lips (lips that can cut?). Moving warily around the room as if apprehensive of something falling on him unexpectedly from the ceiling. Wearing an old brown jersey, a bit too big for him, as if he had grown out of it in reverse. Light trousers, almost like thin canvas, (a sailor's trousers?), torn and vaguely mended with improvised patches at the knees. In his stockings, blue woollen ones with holes in them. His face flecked with an almost adolescent stubble. Someone who has little or no beard, like Njall? But later he shows me a snapshot of him years ago with a fine dark beard, very narrow.

Jessie looks much younger, very nice, very quiet. In a silk almost sheath dress, a little unfashionably short, showing boyish knees. Her hair over her forehead and down her cheeks so that she almost seems to hide behind it. A gentle face, looks barely 15 at times, a few freckles. Is almost deaf in one ear so that walking down the street she'd have to change sides, in an apologetic animal sort of way, in order to hear. Says things are "super" (the ultimate adjective) and "posh" (anything expensive or fancy). Ian also. Both use Scots words all the time. Ian "I was fair scunner't." And Jessie asking me is I'd like a "peeece" so that it took me a moment to remember, my grandmother, "a jeely-piece" (a slice of bread and butter with jam on). Their ultimate disparagement of anyone: "a twit".

I get out my little presents, curiosities for them. Some yucca spikes. Eucalyptus buttons. Then talk with Ian all that afternoon. At first sitting in the window looking out at the backs of the houses opposite. Later, down on the front steps when the sun shifted. The weather now almost suspiciously glorious.

As we sat there, a Corporation man came along, looking puzzled. Asked where the lamp post was. The one usually in front had disappeared since last Friday. Nothing but a little square of dirt where it had been.

Who could have wanted to steal it? He grins at us and shakes his head and wanders off back down the street. Ian and I laughing in great glee, as if we had done it.

Jessie has gone off to work at café nearby, The Partisan, from 4 to 6.30. I go off to find a guest house. Three streets up, by chance, on Northumberland Street, only a few doors from 48 where Ian was previously. On my way back, pass The Alna Press in a basement.

Everyone and everything very close. Tom Scott, Goodsir-Smith, Garioch[2] all live within a few streets. I buy some groceries for high tea. On an impulse, some pork pies. Ian and Jessie laughing at me that they taste awful. But Jessie shyly eats one of the three, then divides the odd one with me. Ian revealing that 3 years ago (so recently? perhaps I misremember slightly) he was writing advertising copy, and for that identical brand of pie!

We talk late, later than I thought, my watch being 1½ hours slow. So that I sleep in the next morning and nearly miss breakfast at the guest house. Out for a walk to taste the air, and then back to 24 Fettes Row. More talk and tea, then I set off for Jim Haynes' bookshop (Paperback, a sort of poets' centre), a small place, rather a shrunken version of City Lights. Almost in the shadow of the Medical School and Royal Infirmary, students from the university about. Haynes himself with a little black goatee and moustache. An American, recently back from New Orleans but no southern accent. Lived many years in South America and speaks perfect Spanish. Came to Edinburgh in 1956 more or less by chance, and stayed. Book shop not very profitable but he is involved in other city projects. Co-director of a theatre club (The Traverse) and also a chairman of the committee for the annual Writer's Conference during the Festival. Last year, The Novel. This year, Drama. Next year to be Poetry, then Philosophy. But he doubts if it may go on past this year, usual money problems. John Calder, the publisher, has backed it.

Haynes trying to draw me out, to convince me that I should stay in Edinburgh. Introducing me to a couple of other friends who wander in, one a pathologist who gives me the name of someone in anaesthesia at the Infirmary. The other, a philosopher, a cheerful little goblin of a

---

[2] Scott (1918-1995), Sydney Goodsir Smith (1915-1975) and Robert Garioch (1909-1981) were all significant forces in Scottish poetry of the 20th century.

man who tells me that he once slept on Arthur's grave at Glastonbury and "wrote a poem" when he woke up in the morning.

Haynes himself vaguely asking me if I'd like to meet some people "in communications... radio and TV" but I'm not sure how specific it is, and not sure if I'd really want to meet them anyway. Off to find a copy of the B.M.J. [re possible job] but can't bring myself to go to see anyone at the Infirmary or Medical School.

Haynes tells me about the plays they are doing that night at his theatre club, and I decide to go. He orders tickets for Jessie and I, but doubts if Ian could be persuaded. (He couldn't be. Can't go out that far and anyway, can't face that kind of *culture*.)

Later, before tea, I keep Ian company when he goes to see his doctor, a couple of streets away, to get another medical certificate. He seems to cope with the streets cheerfully enough but peering about warily. A pointed face, rather like a hungry fox, yet anxious about the hounds. Pointing out a green door across the street where he used to see some Estonian refugee standing in the evenings. "It was like he was in a forest, all alone there, you could right *feel* the trees around him. He wasn't in Edinburgh at all. I have a poem about it." (The word coming out very solemnly "poh-em".)

I eat at 24 with them and then Jessie and I set out back for the theatre, taking the bus. She now in her "posh" dress, with a thin little pink scarf, the dress light blue, very simple. I find her curiously fascinating. Her apparent shyness and yet how much she gets done. Now starting an Art Gallery in the basement of the cafe where she works. Last year they actually had a *shop* in the centre of the city where they sold Wild Hawthorn books. Just during the Festival. Only 30/- week rent. Did quite well. Seem to sell most of their things, even make a profit. She looks embarrassed, like a schoolgirl caught passing a note in class. "But we're so awful at business, there never seems any money for the next book." (I suspect that any extra money soon gets used up on bread and tea, and all the special projects that aren't for sale). Ian draws National Assistance.

After we've picked up the tickets, we (Jessie & I) walk up the Lawnmarket to the Castle Courtyard and look out over the city. At its loveliest for us in the sunny evening. She points out a cannon-ball embedded in the wall of an adjacent house. Laughs when I pronounce *wynd* as "wind" instead of "wined". Back to the Traverse in time for the plays. Telling me about The Poets' Protest March they talked about organising last year.

"We let it out that we'd have a wee zeppelin with us and they believed it! On the radio and all. Quite exciting. Even said we'd have a lorry as autodestructive art, with explosives, to blow itself up. I don't know where they got that. Even on the television. It's fair amazing!" I have a sudden sense of how small everything is, that if I were to pin up a poem on a street corner nearby, half Scotland might know about it in the morning.

Jim Haynes there to greet us at the theatre. I sense a caution in him towards Jessie and Ian. An apprehension about what they *might* do next. The plays are Ionesco's *The Lesson* and Genet's *The Maids*. Very well done. Everything around a central acting area, about 40 seats and 2/3 full.

But I find myself suddenly a little weary of that kind of theatre, of the *effort* that is involved, the constant strain of it, never to let you relax for a moment. How hard the actors are working.

At half time (rather like a rugger match, to give the players a chance to rest) we go upstairs for coffee and cake. Jessie cautious at first about the cake, then wolfing it down. I sense a relief to be away from Ian for just a few hours. Also suspect that she may be just plain hungry. She eats half my piece. We even share puffs on a cigarette. It seems easy and strangely chummy.

The plays over, we go out into the night, still almost light at 10.30. She suggests we walk and it's a good evening for that. But the plays not to her taste. "The second one *frightened* me. I didn't *like* it. It was so *fierce*." And so back to Ian, who has finished a concrete poem while we were out, a nice one about roses and yes and you and us. So to enjoy cocoa and talk until midnight, all of us in a gay mood, poking sly digs at each other and everyone. Back to the guest house in the dark. But I can't sleep, too wound up, hearing 4 a.m. strike.

Nonetheless, wake the next morning quite refreshed. After breakfast, meet Jim Haynes on the street by chance. Blather for a while. He grumbling about the business pressures from some of the wholesalers, their "combine" tactics. Offers me a wine party at the Paperback shop if my book—*A Very Particular Hill*—is done before I leave. (Later, talking

Ian Hamilton Finlay

with Jessie, she thinks this could be arranged as a Reading but the book isn't going to be ready).

So to 24 and it's so warm that the three of us go down into the back yard, a complete shambles of debris, stones from a knocked down wall, like three refugees in the middle of a bombed city. They smoke the cigarettes I brought, but mostly Jessie as Ian rolls one of his own every now and then. I sense a disdain for the ready made ones.

Talking about the theatre and the wireless and kinds of plays. Some Glasgow group are actually doing one of his plays as a Fringe production for the Festival. But currently he is fed up with theatre. "Too many wurrrds". In fact, the fewer words in anything, the better he likes it. Especially hates syntax. Has been wrestling several weeks trying to write a brief introduction for an exhibition of paintings by a local painter he admires. "I get stuck when I have to write a whole sentence. It gets all too complicated." And how he seeks a poetry that will be "pure" ("pyoor"). Yet can write letters easily enough. It's the prose that baulks him. Finally making a sort of diagram instead, for the Introduction, a dozen words, perhaps less, connected by lines.

Of current theatre, saying that "I want it to be beautiful, and pure, and with as few words as possible". Joking that he tried to get the Scottish BBC to broadcast a tape recording of a starry night.

I discover that he isn't from Orkney after all. Only lived there about a year. His wife went up, for some reason, something to do with some friend of hers. Afterwards, they lived for eight years in a small house in Perthshire, she painting and he doing a variety of jobs about the countryside. Prior to that, he had lived in Glasgow. Where he had known MacDiarmid, and been on mildly amiable terms with him. Also Bill Turner. Both of whom I discover he has less enmity towards personally than one might gather from his letters. Finding approving things to say about Turner's latest book of poems. But the only poet in Edinburgh for whom he has any use is Garioch. "Och, he's so Scotch. We might go to see him. He's a funny little man, turribly Scotch, and doesn't say much at all. But nice. Not nasty like everyone else."

We have last meal, Jessie and I shopping for it. A bottle of wine. (Ian doesn't drink at all. "But I do" Jessie hastily adds.) Two cartons of yoghurt. Some lettuce. A tin of crab meat. Jessie cooks up some soup in a cup, her own stock, pieces of potato, fragments of a green leafy vegetable, and shreds of chicken. A feast. With strong tea prepared this time by Ian, with jokes about how many spoons of tea he had put into the pot. Chocolate biscuits to finish.

As I prepare to go, he says to give his love "to everyone… except —— —" and grins, mischievous, but also serious. Jessie tells me that when he was at 48 Northumberland Street, they got the notion to plant some flowers in the barren back garden. Jessie bought a packet of Wild Flower Seeds, and Ian lovingly watered them every day with his tea pot. They came up beautifully. Until the first blossoms came out and the whole garden was full of thistles. They tried to pretend to the landlord that they'd had nothing to do with it.

A last gift to me, of Ian's extra jersey, which I'd been wearing part of the time. All stained and smelly, and out at the elbows. I am hugely delighted.

*

(On my return, a week or so later, I give a little reading at the Paperback. About 20 there, mostly friends of Jim Haynes or Jessie. To my pleasure, Garioch also. A most attentive listener.)

*

[Other notes]

Ian saying, as Jessie and I came in after the reading, and I asked him about the 'Tug Poems' he had been writing, "Oh, I tore them up." At my protest, he says, "I felt they weren't pure (pyooor) enough. I didn't feel I was pure when I wrote them. It's awful". He would pause between phrases. "They made me feel *un*-pure. Perhaps I'm no pure enough any more to write poems." Then, partly to Jessie, "I've no been feeling well. I don't know what it is."

I try to tease him "You'll soon be as bad as —. You have to be really holy to write anything." He grins, "Aye" and looks at me sideways. Then curls up in the big chair, like some animal in its lair. Only his eyes really showing.

(I remember, that first visit: walking back from the Traverse with Jessie, 11 o'clock, but still a soft light, the city drifting into quiet. Slowly down the Mound and into Hanover Street. I saying, "I think you're a masquerade. You pretend to be Miss McGuffie. I've heard about *her*. *She* has a degree in Classics, and keeps Edinburgh in an uproar." And she backs away slightly and swings a kick at me, "You're awful. I'm *that* ashamed sometimes. I *do* have a degree, really. It's as if I'd done something *wrong*."

I ask her if I can see her press cuttings, the piece that was in *The Scotsman* the day before about her row with the other woman over the projected Partisan Gallery. She says she tore them up. "It's that *awful*. And it's all Ian's fault. He phoned the papers himself about it, to *protest*. I wish he *wouldn't*. But he does like to *stir* into things. He stirs them on purpose." And as we walk I see a long finger working around into something rather like thick porridge, and the slightly wicked grin on a face that might be that of a satyr.

The next morning there was a letter from the woman who owns the café, reproaching Jessie in a complicated fashion, full of innuendoes. All something to do with who was to be invited to the opening viewing and who wasn't. Earl Haig being one of those the woman didn't want invited but they did. Jessie: "It's fair depressing. People just go *on* about things. I hate it. I'm not working there anymore. It's as if they just *wanted* to spoil things. And it would have been a *super* place."

They'd already had a programme printed, in offset, for the Peter Stitt pictures. With a concrete poem of Ian's as Introduction.)

*

Midnight, the gas fire hissing, Ian curled up in the chair with a light behind his head (red fabric shade on it with a wire frame, all hanging in tatters) and Jessie on the floor at the other side, sitting with her legs folded under her. Ian looking up at the near corner of the mantelpiece, Jessie out towards the darkened window, and I lying on my back looking up at the ceiling, my head a foot from Jessie's knees. (The ceiling has a pattern of diamond dots which has a strange effect, as if the surface was rippling, and I remark that "I can say one day that I lay on Miss McGuffie's floor and watched the ceiling go up and down." Jessie: "You're awful".)

*

More Words

There were long and cosy silences, as if the three of us were drifting with the room through the night, on some far off ocean or as if in a bed time story. And as Ian talks, I have the sense of a long and very thin wedge, the tip of which he has inserted under some edifice called *Poetry in Scotland* and every word is another tap on that wedge, which he is driving home, slowly but irresistibly. So that one can feel the whole country tremble slightly, every so often, hardly realising what is happening to it.

On the wall are some newspaper headlines cut out and stuck on cardboard saying "Lobster Refloated".

Ian surprises me by asking about Robert Kelly[3], whom I don't know. Earlier, Jessie had asked about "wee Ronald" who had visited them. "I was fair taken with him. He gave us some *super* poems." This was Ronald Johnson[4], at that time Jonathan William's companion, and she occasionally mentioned him later, always "wee Ronald". It must have been his quietness and gentleness. I tell her how much, in fact, he hadn't liked Britain generally, and was glad to get back to America. She wonders if this was all the walking. "Aye, Jonathan does like to *walk* so. We got postcards from him, from the Lakes."

Then I confess how wrong I had been, on my earlier visit, about Coronado, when I had corrected something in one of Ronald's poems, that Coronado *had* reached as far north as Kansas. Ian and Jessie laugh in glee. "Aye, you were that!" Because I had been so "superior" when I had corrected it.

Ian goes most afternoons down a few doors to Cyril Barrow's place. Barrow was an original, with tawny beard and hollow cheeks and shaggy black hair and a very London accent, so that when I first met him I thought for a moment that he was imitating Pete Brown[5], which sounded very bizarre in Edinburgh. With a cheerful young wife and new baby. He had been an engineer but drifted into the book trade, second-hand and rare editions, now with a growing overdraft.

---

[3] Robert Kelly (b. 1935) American poet. Author of over 50 books of poetry and prose.
[4] Ronald Johnson (1935-1998), American poet. Best-known for the long poems *ARK* and *RADI OS*, the latter an erasure of *Paradise Lost*.
[5] Pete Brown (b. 1940), English poet, songwriter and singer. Published by Fulcrum Press in the 1960s, he is today best-known for having written the lyrics for many songs by Cream (1966-68).

Barrow has some joiners' tools at his flat and Ian uses them to make toys. Model aeroplanes, trees, boats, even a toy tomb ("tooom", and very proud of this) One huge construction, meant to be a water wheel and mill, with lots of space to pour water in and nowhere, except the carpet, for it to run out into. All of them painted cheerful colours. As a parting gift, I am allowed to chose one of the two tugs with barges. He is saving the other to show some friend of theirs, now in California, a girl named Leslie. For some unknown reason, it is essential that she should see all his toys before he sells them.

The talk drifts to lollipops, one of the toys being a lollipop forest. And there are plans for a special Sweet Issue of POTH, with "sweet" poems, and a free lollipop with each copy. Jessie: "But Ian won't see that they'll get sticky and mess up the issue". The problem being that wrapped lollipops cost too much.

*

He feels little or no interest any more in his plays or stories, even the earlier poems, even those in *Whistling in the Dark*[6]. I tell him that there's only sculpture left, that that is what his toys are leading towards. In fact, already are.

Another time, talking with Jessie she asks what my plans are and I talk of how much I've enjoyed being back in Edinburgh. Then say, "But perhaps it's just Ian, not anything else. And I suppose if I stayed here long enough I'd only end up having some colossal row with him. Still, even having Ian to row with would be something." And a grave look comes over her face, and a wariness, as she says, "It's not *nice* having a row with Ian. He *hits* people."

In the room, I'd said how hard it was for me to learn to do nothing, and perhaps how important it is, and Ian says "Aww, Jessie's guid at that, she is that." And Jessie shakes her bangs in annoyance, and then sighs. "I am... I'm just super at doing nothing." Then Ian, "I bet there aren't many who could beat Jessie at doing nothing." And Jessie, "I do it for days, sometimes. It's awful. You don't know." And as I look over,

---

[6] An early pamphlet of twelve poems from Wild Hawthorn Press.

her cigarette is burning down in her left hand, her attention suddenly elsewhere, as if she had suddenly escaped from us.

Letter to *The English Intelligencer*

Thanks for sending me *The English Intelligencer*[1] – but I'm hard put to know what sort of reply I can make – at the same time, it would seem to require *some* sort of acknowledgement – I don't know, maybe I'm all wet etc., but I just don't see the point of such near parodies of Olson as, for example, that first poem – I mean, I'm interested to see what Temple[2] can do with his "roots" etc. – but must he swipe the means *so* obviously from Olson? – I can't believe this is really what Olson intended, anyway – I know, it's easy to carp, and easy to be negative, etc., but the whole thing seems to me to be an easy transcript into what is the currently fashionable American poetic idiom – OK, I agree, it's *been* very much alive and interesting, and it's damn hard to get past it – but, but, surely, somehow, there *are* ways of being "for the island and its language" without merely parroting what certain Americans have done (and done very well)? – even so many American poets are now imitating what *was* original and alive 15 years ago – not that I have much (if any) alternative to offer – but at least it should be possible to avoid the more obvious sorts of "I, minimus, of West Hartlepool etc." – or the nervous jerks of Creeleyesque – heck, there are even more possibilities in American speech than *that* (however effective and interesting it may be –

> "what *are* you wearing
> underneath those jeans?"
> —Barry MacSweeney, 'To Ann' (1:1. [6])[3]

But each to his own grindstone – and you are trying to prod something to happen – and luck to you in that – it's just that, somehow, I had hoped for something else – what, I must admit, I'm not sure – and I do realize that, trying to edit a magazine, it takes several issues sometimes to establish what one is after –

---

[1] *The English Intelligencer* was a periodical circulated free of charge to interested parties. It was edited from Cambridge by Andrew Crozier (first series) and Peter Riley (second series) in 1966-68. This letter, the first received by *TEI*, was published in series 1, issue 3 (1966).
[2] John Temple (b. 1942). His *Collected Poems* was published by Salt in 2003.
[3] The number reference here indicates that the quote is taken from a poem which appeared in the *Intelligencer*, Series 1, issue 1, page 6.

But, as Lucie-Smith[4] remarked at Nottingham, I am probably a "quietist" and a "personalist" – I haven't much sense of "the island and its language" – my only sense is of this individual or that individual, with his or her voice, discrete and each themselves – and I look to a Robert Garioch[5], or a Jonathan Williams[6], or a Tom Pickard[7] – each speaks his own tongue, and makes his own poems, as best he can – I hope this island *doesn't* have a language, in a sense – I must confess that I admire many of Philip Larkin's poems –

But enough, if not too much, and excuse all the "negative" response – but I wanted to try to say how it struck me – relevant or not –

[An editorial note is appended to the letter, saying that "Dr Turnbull has been invited to contribute a note on the poems of Tom Pickard".]

---

[4] Edward Lucie-Smith (b. 1933), poet, editor, artist, photographer and art historian. Edited the influential and—in its first edition—*inclusive* anthology, *British Poetry Since 1945* for Penguin Books (1970), where Gael Turnbull's work featured, with Roy Fisher and Basil Bunting, alongside more predictable names for the time.
[5] Robert Garioch (1909-1981), Scottish poet and translator, who wrote in both Scots and English.
[6] Jonathan Williams (1929-2008), American poet, photographer, and influential publisher of The Jargon Society press from North Carolina.
[7] See note 5 on p.47.

Arabic and Persian Poems
by Omar Pound[1]

Arabic and Persian, but they are Omar Pound's poems. Translations? But any poem must start somewhere. Be it all anecdote, a personal experience, a turn of phrase or a rhythmical pattern. Or someone else's poem. And the poaching here is done from the classical literature of the Persian and Arabic-speaking worlds. From 500 to 1400 A.D. With a happy lack of false scruple, using whatever happens to be useful "…a few lines from one poem, a restatement of a point of view in another … occasionally the personal and historical circumstances … and always Western literary and social allusions…"

Some obvious comments. Little or no use of the original verse forms. The impact of the poem is dependent upon the thrust and concision of the phrasing. From Al-Hutay'a:

It is new
therefore a pleasure,

and death?
is that also
cordial
and sugar?

Not too much concern to differentiate the tone of this or that poet, or this or that era, or even between the Persian and Arabic. From Samarqandi, a Persian and 400 years later than the previous:

I leave to you
the public's taste
for sorrel, vinegar
and human waste.

Which is not meant as any complaint about lack of variety. On the contrary. If the most successful of the poems are probably those which have a wry or mocking edge, there is the gentleness and pathos of this from Ibn Hazm:

---

[1] Omar Pound *Arabic & Persian Poems* (London: Fulcrum Press 1970). Republished as *Arabic and Persian Poems in English* (Orono, ME: National Poetry Foundation 1985).

More Words

> I have no guide
> no calendar inside
> except a smile
> and little kiss
> she gave me
> by surprise
> upon my brow.
>
> And now,
> that little while
> is all my life
> and all reality,
> how long or brief
> it seems to be.

The most technically accomplished of all the poems is a narrative piece, 'Calling the Doctor', from Arudi. Really a short story? Done in seven sections, full of vivid detail, with continually shifting pace and tone. Jesting and affectionate by turn. Character, era, incident, humour and drama, wit and poetry enough for most books, crammed into some hundred and twenty lines.

Many are essentially dramatic, or imply a drama which does not need further explanation. This, from Rumi:

> I cry:
> but you want comforting
>
> I am silent:
> you hope for tears
>
> I joust:
> 'keep still' you say
>
> and in my lassitude
> you'd have me up and do.
>
> Why this autumn chill
> where I expected Spring?

'Arabic & Persian Poems' by Omar Pound

There is also a fifteen page account of both Arabic and Persian literature, comprehensive and full of careful detail, with extensive notes on individual poets and a bibliography. It is possible to enjoy the poems and ignore the scholarship if that is your taste. Or, vice versa. Or, savour the counterpoint. Accomplishment enough on both sides.

A few minor grumbles. Some of the titles for the poems are wildly distracting. (Often, one suspects, intentionally.) The sequence of notes on the poets appears (as far as I could puzzle it out) to bear no relationship to the sequence of the poems. (True, an irrelevance—if the poems bear little relationship to the individual poets to whom they are ascribed?) Occasional efforts to be overly subtle miss their mark. I find it hard to think:

> oh god, live for ever
> young and beautiful

anything other than banal, even if it is intentionally so as an old man's sentimentality. And so on.

But at the very least, Allah be praised, never dull. Or pompous. And though I have emphasized to what extent these are Omar Pound's poems, yet he has often caught something which rings true across the barriers of language, culture and time. This, from Minuchihri, one poet to another:

> I send you my verses
> citing passion without passion,
> three this week and two before.
>
> Perhaps you do not like the stuff
> or blush. Your silence
> gives me no excuse for more.

I can't imagine many readers experiencing such a "silence". In his foreword, "To the reader", he says, "My aim: a readable poem and a rediscovery." And for me, bang on target.

A Soundproof Gesture
published August 1982 by Migrant Press

A Soundproof Gesture Selected Poems by Hugh Creighton Hill
200 numbered copies. Cover design by Jon Gamble. 24 pages. £1

These twenty-nine poems have been selected by Gael Turnbull and Philip Sharpe, in collaboration with the author, and represent a cross-section of Hill's writing since about 1950. They are taken from *Some Propositions from the Universal Theorem* (Artisan, 1954) *Hill's Epitaphs* (Tarasque, 1952 & 1968) and *Latterday Chrysalides* (Migrant, 1961) as well as from an unpublished collection *Cuts* (circa 1967) and a number of previously uncollected or unpublished poems.

Born in 1906 in Widnes, near Liverpool, where he has spent most of his life, his early work appeared in *Poetry* (Chicago) under Harriet Monroe and later editors, and attracted the occasional attention of writers as diverse as Aldous Huxley, T.S. Eliot and Robert Graves, and, in the early 1950s, Charles Olson. In *The Maximus Poems*, 'Letter Five', Olson remarks:

> "not even Hugh Hill, whose triangles
> are so nicely made but the course he's running
> doesn't strike me as good enough
> to come home a winner…"

Olson would seem to have done so but whatever the judgement of history and however one may determine "a winner", at the very least Hugh Hill held his course and even Olson was impressed, however much at variance.

In one of the untitled later poems, Hill states it clearly enough:

> All those people in *The Yellow Book*
>   and *New Writing*
> but they didn't go on to do anything
>
> Why?

The question is crucial. The answer is also, and worth having and clearly given: there is no answer. Either you do or you don't. And in his sometimes crabbed, sometimes almost perverse way, Hugh Creighton

Hill did, and does "go on". Often even in spite of his preoccupation with a sense that he had failed to achieve what he had before him to achieve. It has narrowed the range of his attention, the material with which he works, as it has probably served to sharpen his attention within that limitation.

At an age when most writers might have given up at the lack of any public success or retired into a self-satisfied rut, he continued to refine and develop and invent. He has been consistently indifferent to fashion (if not to fame) but never indifferent to the demands of the precept "Make It New". As he remarked thirty years ago—with thirty years of writing already behind him:

> If life is learning
> my ignorance increases.

It is easy and tempting to make exaggerated claims for a neglected craftsman but there can be few poets who have so consistently increased the compression and passion—and detached wit and savage humour—of their poems, long after most of their publicly applauded contemporaries have lapsed into silence or indulgent repetition. After a lifetime of sustained commitment with little more than scattered and occasional publication, the poems have survived and will survive.

> . . . pebbles in the water
> making a soundproof gesture
>   against all arsy versy
>   paddy-pawed charlatans

A Letter to Sylvia Price Turner

Dear Sylvia,

What follows will be mostly familiar to you, and indeed, you may be able to correct me in places.

I first came into contact with Bill about the time I returned to Britain in the autumn of 1955, or a few months later. Why I first wrote to him, I can't recall. Perhaps he even wrote to me? There may be a relevant letter somewhere.

He was then living at 108 Elder St, Glasgow, SW1. The link was his activity as editor of a little magazine, called with characteristic assurance and directness: *The Poet*, probably recommended to me by a friend. He was proud, with good reason, that by laborious hand setting and printing it himself, he actually ran it at a very slight profit, even paid contributors. His choice of poems was both catholic (a wide range of styles and from across the entire English-speaking world) and stringent (the *reputation* of any poet meant nothing, or what was currently fashionable).

I never visited him at that time but we began a friendship (by correspondence) that continued, with occasional lulls, for the rest of his life.

I came across a letter, entirely by chance, 25 years later, relevant to those years in Glasgow. How and why it survived and then turned up where and how it did, I cannot explain. It was marked CONFIDENTIAL and was from a Government Training Centre, Industrial Rehabilitation Unit, Glasgow, dated 9 April 1949, and includes "It is reported that he has considerable literary and poetic talent but no direct evidence of this was given here. When he came to us he had been unemployed for some time and was rather bitter about the Ministry of Labour and life in general." My other glimpse of his life then was from an American poet who visited him, and reported how horrified he was at the cold (lack of fuel), very basic sanitation, and the surroundings.

Bill was extremely generous to me and on his own initiative (with his choice of poems) published a pamphlet for me in his *Cameo* series, *A Libation*, in 1957. He wisely overruled my first bizarre suggestion in regard to the cover, and indeed often made useful and stimulating comments on my work.

He had no use for many of the poets who interested *me* at the time, but this did not seem to matter, and I both respected and admired his own poems, particularly the sharpness of language and detail. One of these from later years remains for me as a touchstone, that exemplifies something essential as to what poetry is about, the 'Mexican Jumping Bean', though Bill himself, as I recall, did not particularly value it. (This may have been merely the mood of a moment, as I note that his comments at the back of my copy imply a bitterness that it had been unfairly slighted.)

When I was briefly an editor myself I was pleased to be able to use one of his little satires, on the Scottish poetry scene. He had little use for MacDiarmid, and only scorn for those who idealised him.

We finally met in the summer of 1963. I was then living in California, and came over on a visit. Going south from seeing friends in Edinburgh, it was natural to call on him where he was then in Leeds (where he had been a Gregory Fellow) and was managing a precarious living doing some part time teaching, as well as writing. I remember being greatly impressed with the two boys, and his pride in them. Also, his interest in board games. I particularly recall playing one involving racing cars.

We next met in Glasgow, about 1966 or '67, where he had a flat, and income as some sort of writer in residence connected with the University. He was very happy, by then separated or divorced, with a new relationship (a former student, I believe) and work that satisfied. He enjoyed being the non-academic (even anti-academic) who had "made it" in that world, and knew more about the actual writing of poems than most of the professors. His practical future, always independent and on his own terms, appeared if not absolutely assured, at least likely to continue more or less as it had done over the previous ten years.

My next memory is calling on him in London, nearly ten years or so later. He was alone, depressed, and in considerable financial difficulty. In fact, I believe that he had slept rough more than once. As it happened, I had a flat available in Malvern. This had been bought by and for my parents to use but circumstances had changed, and the friend who had been staying in it temporarily had just left. I suggested that Bill use it, at nominal rent. So he came.

Unfortunately, in spite of a lot of damp-proofing work, the flat remained resolutely damp. There was even a live (and not just metaphorical) frog at one point. In general, after an initial euphoria, Bill was not greatly taken with Malvern, nor Malvern with him. However, he did make one enduring friend there, Tony Dash, also an exile and only waiting to get away.

I would see him fairly regularly for a chat, mostly writing gossip, and occasional practical concerns. He had given up trying to write potboiler thrillers, at which he had been modestly successful, finding that the immense work involved was out of all proportion to the practical rewards, and that he was as well off on whatever unemployment benefit he could get. I remember he did do occasional work for the BBC, but it was a bleak period in his life. The death of his son Leslie shook him deeply, especially since he had long ago lost contact with Kenneth who had gone to America.

There were various girlfriends (none locally of significance) who sometimes came to stay, and my memory is that by then he lived when they came, endured when alone again. One of them, a student from Edinburgh and young enough to be his daughter, wanted to marry him but, probably wisely, he declined. He didn't have much use for my circle of friends and activities and I think that when he was finally offered a post as writer-in-residence with the library service, based at Bedford, it was a relief for both of us. There was a flat that went with the post, and I hired a van to take a load of his possessions over there for him, in the late summer of 1979.

Our lives have mostly diverged since but it has been wonderful to see him settled and happy at last in Lincoln. I notice that I have put that in the present tense. Which is not altogether inappropriate. Even as the words "settled" and "happy" do not apply easily, at least to my sense of him, with so much that was restless, often frustrated, at odds with the world, even perhaps with himself. Although there can be few who have so consistently pursued their own course, whatever the difficulties. And who achieved so much, and was, amid the constraints of his own needs, so generous in what he gave to others.

William Price Turner (1927-1998): An Appreciation

William Price Turner published under the name "W. Price Turner" until about 1979, when he began to use "Bill Turner", the label under which he had published the last five of the six novels—thrillers—which gave him some precarious income for a few years.

Most of his personal life, including periods as Gregory Fellow at Leeds and writer-in-residence at Glasgow, is not relevant to this appreciation but some understanding of his early years is helpful. Although born in York, his parents returned to their native Scotland when he was still an infant. Forced to leave formal education when only 14, he grew up, and spent his early adult years, in Glasgow, and throughout his life, in his words, was "permanently encumbered by a Scottish accent".

From 1951 to 1957, still in Glasgow, he edited and hand printed 15 issues of *The Poet*, a truly "little magazine", and was justly proud of its quality and international scope, and that it featured early poems by names later to become well known.[1]

Throughout his life he published regularly in magazines, wrote occasional reviews and other items, and had plays and poems broadcast. In later years he found amusement, as well as income, winning poetry and verse competitions (entered anonymously). Mostly rebuffed by major publishers, his books and pamphlets in fact sold well. The only one still in print is *Fables for Love, New and Selected Poems* (Peterloo, 1985).

His first full collection was *The Rudiment of an Eye* (1955) where the most achieved poem is probably 'Idealist', but the opening lines from 'Egotist' give a more immediate impression of some major characteristics: the use of imagery, the compression and sharpness of phrasing, and an element of mockery amid celebration.

> I have a rage trained
> on many an old hurt,
> but I do not feed it;
> I keep it chained
> in a sly cellar
> where it snarls at its own smell.

---

[1] See account in *Poetry Matters* (Peterloo, Autumn 1984) [Author's note.]

The Flying Corset (1962) is notable for more overtly satirical pieces (the three 'Kilroy' villanelles being particularly accomplished) flashing with what one reviewer remarked as "progressive energy". The title poem starts:

> At last, the flying corset, the first
> manufactured garment to give genuine uplift,
> tested and certified, as real as thirst,
> and as exhilarating to indulge...

The device is sustained for 77 lines, making a virtuoso elaboration of the central metaphor, and using it as a commentary on the human situation, mixing derision with wry understanding: should we laugh or despair?

Another good example of his use of metaphor (and ironic fantasy) is the title poem of *The Moral Rocking-Horse* (1970) which begins:

> Wanted: Good Home for Moral Rocking-Horse.
> I just fell off again. It's clear
> my riding days are strictly limited,
> but that unbreakable brute
> needs exercise I can't maintain.

The poem ends with the comment of a bystander:

> in honest puzzlement:
> *But it gets you nowhere.*
> And that's perfectly true.
> I wonder where he wanted to go.

Of the newer poems in *Fables for Love* the most striking, for invention and elaboration, are 'Cuckoo Clock and Camera: A Dialogue', and 'A Prune Named Wittgenstein' which imagines the master reincarnated as a prune speaking to his disciple Rodney:

> If you knew how I long to be assimilated!
> Yet I fear that your logical tapeworm
> may urge you to deny me. Rodney, I could
> explain everything, but it would take too long.

> Consider how Leibnitz and Newton's protracted
> debate sent God to sleep...

and goes on to range across the problems and paradoxes of thought and human frailty, ending with:

> ...has not your meekest student
> advised you where you can shove Wittgenstein?

Not included in this volume is his 'Mexican Jumping Bean' which he categorised as "a longish poem". The bean is, of course, not a bean but a chrysalis and becomes both the subject and characterisation of a poem which he sustains and varies for 264 compact lines that twitch with impudent energy.

Not all his work is so emblematic. There are many lyrical pieces (his Glasgow poems and 'The Back Court Piper' sequence) but also direct and personal poems charged with intense feeling, particularly 'Visitation', 'Progress Report', 'Reproaches', 'As Advertised' and 'Idealist'. These do not easily lend themselves to excerpts, depending on a sustained structure for their effect.

Much ignored in his later years, and bypassed by the vagaries of literary fashion, his poems remain among the most individual and obsessively crafted of any written in English in the past half century.

John Adlard: A Memoir and an Appreciation

"Some, perhaps, will read,
Some, perhaps, listen..."

Toward the end of 1981 or very early in 1982, I received five poems in the post. These came from a friend who published occasional pamphlets and to whom they had been submitted, who suggested that I might find them of interest, although unsuitable for his purposes. The group was under the general title of 'The Names of Places' and four of them, although not in the same grouping, eventually appeared in *The Dance of the Blessed Spirits*, published in 1988. I was immediately struck by the condensation and simplicity of language, the energy and control of pace under an apparently casual tone, as well as, in last word of the title poem, their dignity.

I did not recognise the name of the poet, John Adlard, although we discovered later that we had shared the pages of the same magazine in 1971; and I had forgotten his earlier association with the Oxford magazine, *Departure*. I wrote to him in the New Year and the first of many laconic letters arrived, dated 23 January 1982, thanking me for my interest.

His next letter was longer and recorded a few personal details including his marriage in 1981, and that he had published mostly prose and translations. With his permission, I sent copies of 'The Names of Places' to a couple of friends who edited magazines, to try to interest them, but without success.

In May he sent me a longer and more formal sequence, of which I did not keep a copy, and on which I made some comments and criticisms. This was shortly before he had his accident in Ireland. After he was home from the hospital in August, I had a letter disagreeing with some, but not all, of my suggestions and continuing the correspondence. Sometimes he sent poems, as I did, or pamphlets, or items from magazines. Occasionally there were just postcards, often of the nature of: "Nothing interesting to tell you. Things get nowhere. All the best for everything. John. 4/5/86".

In the autumn of 1983, he sent his 'Sobieski in Autumn', which I admired enormously. I suggested that it might benefit from a more attractive cover and arranged to buy 100 copies from the original publisher. These were eventually circulated, mostly to friends, under a new cover with a drawing by a friend of his.

It was while collecting these copies that we finally met in May 1984. This was, at his arranging, on the steps of the British Museum. My wife was with me. He was alone. It was a warm day, and he was dressed very casually, wearing sandals and carrying a briefcase containing papers. We had coffee in the museum restaurant.

Other than his limp, two things struck us and which changed very little on two subsequent meetings. One was a social awkwardness, and difficulty maintaining any "back and forth" exchange in the conversation. The other was something hard to ignore yet seemingly cruel or unfair to describe: the condition of his mouth. I presume that he had a pathological fear of dentists, or even a phobia about toothbrushes; or it may have been largely the effects of poverty.

Whatever the reason, it was distressing, and to him as well. On the last of our three meetings, in Edinburgh in 1991, where he had come to direct a summer language school, his self-consciousness about it was increasingly painful and he would repeatedly try to cover his mouth with his hand. It cannot have helped his sense of isolation and more specifically, his hopes for another relationship after the break-up of his marriage. A postcard, dated 13/3/87, records: "Terrible things are happening. Emiko [is] insisting on a divorce."

But surmounting these details, my image of him was and still is that of one of Helen Waddell's "wandering scholars", strayed out of a timeless past into a world which does not value integrity or a reverence for words. Probably the world never did. And it was for and through his words that I knew him, and above all, his poems.

One of the shortest is 'Open':

My love, do you remember Lydia Bridge?
We took a shaded path beside a stream,
Entered a church where every door was open.

The first two lines might be the start of any poem of nostalgia, of the character of "love, do you remember?", and the images of the bridge, the "shaded path by a stream", even the "church", no more than a predictable pastoral scene. But "where every door was open", while

More Words

making the simplest of statements, opens the poem into something else, which we may understand as far, or in whatever way we choose, literally or metaphorically; and yet without any pressure to do so, indeed, almost the reverse.

Of course, such poetry does not always succeed, or for all readers, and is certainly not designed to draw attention to itself. Also a succession of simple statements can sometimes be no more than that. Yet he could use concision in a more pointed, more razor-edged and directed way, as in 'The Lichfield Elegy', number 19:

> "We've freed you," smiles the stylish cleverdick,
> "And opened up the land to enterprise.
> They snare us daily with their rhetoric
> And though you may not notice they tell lies.
>
> And while the rich have freedom to compete
> The poor, too, lead enterprising lives.
> They rob us in the daylight in the street.
> They use knives.

One of the poems I first read in MS in 1981/82 is entitled 'Water Eaton', and is more complex in structure than was apparent to me on first encounter:

> Try to reduce the rhythm
> Of the slow summer days and the dark river
> To a pattern of words,
>
> Remembering the girl
> Who whispered to you: *Never be afraid*
> *Of pleasure.*
>
> The water chuckling underneath the prow.
>
> Do not misunderstand
> The kind and constant river:
> Pleasure is not a cistern but a spring.

Line seven, with only a participle, and as a stanza on its own, is unusual. His syntax is normally conventional; but in this instance the context supplies the connections. "Prow" implies the boat, without need of statement, and there is the resonance that what "the girl" whispers may also be what the water is "chuckling." There is also the aptness of "chuckling": both as expression for the sound of water under the prow of a boat but also for the noise of sexual pleasure especially by a woman, a subdued laughter in the throat.

There is also the avoidance of an easy ending, the final line shifting from the river to the antithesis between "cistern" and "spring" while continuing the liquid, and thus implicitly sexual imagery. (It is also interesting that, by mistake, an earlier version of this appeared in a small pamphlet in 1990, without line nine and with the less subtle "taught you" instead of "whispered to you", showing how carefully measured and worked are what often appear almost casual effects.)

I don't know the source of 'The Old Scholar's Song', if it has one specifically, but there is the quality of a translation or version of a poem from another language, perhaps written by an earlier incarnation of John Adlard. Here the pattern of vowel rhymes is beautifully achieved within the laconic structure:

Sensual is wise,
But I—to my hurt—
Was not allowed to know.

Years cantered by;
Family, school, church,
Lovers, friends, foes

Made their demands. I
Was never left alone with words.
Others wrote the poems.

He certainly resented the oppressions of penury and isolation, all the impediments and distractions, practical and emotional, that got in the way of his writing; but that "others wrote the poems", if true to the context of this particular poem, was not true for him.

I had one glimpse, not necessarily typical, of the world where he was forced to earn what he could. I was expecting to be in London briefly and, not sure whether I would have time to meet him or not, made an arrangement that if I did not turn up by a certain time where he was working, he was not to wait for me. As it happened, I thought I would be on time but my train was slightly late and then the taxi was held up in the traffic. When I arrived, he had gone.

It was an address in Soho, a doorway between shops, with a shabby stair, and sign giving the name of a language school. Upstairs, off a barren corridor, were various small rooms. A glimpse suggested scarcely more than a table and two chairs in each. I knocked on some doors and eventually two men appeared, as if surprised that anyone should turn up, telling me that I had just missed him. I had the impression that it was all done by casual appointment, cash in hand. It was as if I had blundered into a Conrad or le Carré novel.

Despite his poverty and loneliness, he found time to help others less fortunate even than himself. A last postcard near the end of 1992, expresses delight to have one of his poems included in a recent anthology by Fiona Pitt-Kethley but mostly asks for practical advice for a Bosnian refugee he was trying to help to resume her studies in Britain.

I replied with what information I had. Then, hearing nothing, though I sent a card at Christmas, thought no more of it, since there were often gaps of several months in our correspondence. I did not see the obituaries and was stunned when the news finally came to me that he was dead.

He wrote many poems, and more and better in his last years. If the world has mostly ignored them, that is the world's loss. For his friends and a few discerning readers, they survive. There may be many more as yet unpublished; and if this memoir may seem to devote a disproportionate amount of space to quotation of and comment on the poems, this is merely to salute what was central to his life, and what I first admired, and will return to, long after personal memories and anecdotes may have faded.

That last postcard, dated 24/11/92, ends, "I hope all is well with you. John."

Remarks on Some Poems by Emily Pfeiffer: A Reconsideration

I.

This paper directs attention to certain specific poems and parts of poems by Emily Pfeiffer, to the general high quality of these poems, and in particular to their interest for feminist criticism; it is is not intended as a full bibliographic or biographic survey. In her own time (1824?–1890) Pfeiffer's work appears to have sold fairly well and it received qualified praise; at least two of her eight collections went into second editions. Two years before her death, Oscar Wilde, in a general review of the women poets of the nineteenth century, praised Elizabeth Barrett Browning and Emily Brontë, from the earlier years, while deprecating Christina Rossetti. He then went on to name some of the more recent women poets "[who] have done really good work", while emphasising Mrs. Browning's influence. His list starts with Emily Pfeiffer.[1]

The entry in the *DNB* (1909) states that she resembled Mrs. Browning. "With incomparably less power [but] uplifted by the same moral ardour and guided by the same delicate sensitiveness… Her defects are those of her predecessor—diffuseness and insufficient finish".[2] *British Authors of the Nineteenth Century* (1936) echoes this judgement. "Her poetry, somewhat suggestive of Mrs. Browning's, has small value for all its high moral worth…"[3] *The Feminist Companion to English Literature* (1990) does note her commitment to women's rights;[4] and Kathleen Hickok in a recent assessment comments that "her poetry evidences a mature, feminist perspective on women's lives and problems"[5] but significantly does not single out any particular poems for their quality as poems.

Columbia Grainger's *Index to Poetry Anthologies* (1990) lists only a single poem by Pfeiffer in the almost 400 poetry anthologies tabulated.

---

[1] Oscar Wilde, 'Poetesses of the Nineteenth Century', from *Queen*, 8 December 1888, reprinted in *Aristotle at Afternoon Tea* ed. John Wyse Jackson, (London, 1991) p.63. [This, and all subsequent footnotes are the author's.]
[2] *Dictionary of National Biography*, (London, 1909) Volume XX, pp.1025–26.
[3] Stanley J. Kunitz and Howard Haycraft, *British Authors of the Nineteenth Century* (New York, 1936) p.495.
[4] *The Feminist Companion to English Literature* (London, 1990) p. 848.
[5] Kathleen Hickok, 'Emily Jane Davis Pfeiffer' in *Dictionary of British Women Writers* (London, 1989) pp. 535–536.

This is 'A Song of Winter' from Gwyn Jones' *Oxford Book of Welsh Verse in English* (1977) which shows her at her most derivative. Christopher Ricks' *New Oxford Book of Victorian Verse* (1987) does not include any of her work.

I would suggest that there are about two dozen poems which deserve rescue from obscurity and which can stand comparison with the best writers of her time. The bulk of them probably do deserve the neglect which followed her death but fashions and perceptions in regard to the appreciation of poems change and we may now see qualities in her best work which her contemporaries or immediate successors did not.

II.

Pfeiffer was born as Emily Jane Davis, probably in Wales and on 26 November 1824.[6] Her father, said to have been an army officer and bankrupt former land owner, was also a painter[7] who encouraged her artistic interests. According to the *DNB* and a slightly earlier biographer[8] she grew up in an atmosphere of genteel poverty and was largely self-educated. In 1850,[9] she married a German businessman based in London and was living in Putney when she died, after being widowed only a year. There were no surviving children and there is no reference in her work to any being born.

---

[6] When she died, 23 January 1890, her death certificate records, on the information of her sister, that she was 65. *General Register Office, St. Catherine's House, London.* Combining this with the birthday in the *DNB*, gives a date of 26 November 1824, possibly at her mother's family home at Milford House, near Newtown, Montgomeryshire. The date of 1827 given by the *DNB* would appear to be wrong.

[7] Pfeiffer's will, with letter by her husband, mentions paintings by her father which were to be kept in the family. *Probate Department, Somerset House, London.*

[8] There is an earlier biographic account, longer than the one in the *DNB*, by Alexander H. Japp, *Poets and Poetry of the Nineteenth Century* edited by Alfred H. Miles (New York, 1907). It is not clear as to where or how he obtained his information or if he had known her personally. He gives a slightly different date for her death and a totally erroneous one for her birth. Hickok's biographic and bibliographic notice in *Dictionary of British Women Writers* (1989) is more complete and bibliographically accurate than the entry in the *DNB*, but otherwise appears to rely on it.

[9] This was at Fyfield, near Abingdon, Berkshire, on 26 January 1850. (The *DNB* wrongly states 1853) Her father, Thomas Richard Davis, and one of her sisters, Caroline, were among the witnesses. *General Register Office.*

Although claimed as Welsh, there is nothing to indicate that she spent much time there or identified with Wales.[10] According to both early biographical sources she spent some formative time in Germany and certainly she had at least a sound knowledge of German. There is evidence of other travel abroad, and in her poems of frequent visits to Scotland.[11]

She published a travel book, a book of essays (reprinted from magazines) *Women and Work*. There is also a prose fantasy written when she was still only 30 and before she had begun to write poems seriously, and a full length play in blank verse, not performed in her life-time.

As well as the shorter poems, Pfeiffer wrote several longer verse narratives, romantic and melodramatic, of a genre popular at the time. The most ambitious, 'The Rhyme of the Lady of the Rock' (1884), alternates the verse stanzas with a prose narrative setting the occasion for the recitation of the poem. The location is Scottish, Duart Castle and the Sound of Mull, with considerable local background; and there is conscious projection and exploration, in the prose sections, of the role of a woman as poet or even *bard*. Hickok finds this of interest from the perspective of the situation of women in the arts in that era but the overall result, although significant as an attempt, is hampered by the obvious influence of Walter Scott.

'Glan-Alarch — His silence and song' (1877) seems even less successful, a book length narrative in blank verse which begins:

I am Glan-Alarch, he who sings
Beneath the morning cloud which wraps Crag Eyrie,
Who basks upon his sun-kiss'd side at noon,
And sleeps with him in silence...[12]

However, there is a rhythmically interesting 'Song' by the minstrel/bard at the end.

---

[10] One of her long narratives, 'Glan-Alarch', does have a patriotically Welsh setting. There are actually more Scottish references in her poems, even some use of Lowland Scots; but the bulk of her work is consistent with the background of an educated and well-travelled upper-middle class English woman of the mid-Victorian period.

[11] Toward the end of her life, she had a married sister living near Aberdeen and one at Smyrna, in Asia Minor, as well as her husband's brother in Wisconsin, U.S.A., and other relatives by marriage in Germany. *Somerset House*.

[12] Pfeiffer, *Glan-Alarch—His silence and song* (London 1877) p.1

III.

One much earlier narrative, 'Margaret; or, The Motherless' (1861), is technically more ambitious and skilful using a variety of stanzaic forms, sometimes speaking through the voice of the protagonist, and containing lively sections.

The story is told obliquely and some details are not explicit, possibly due to the constraints of writing in 1860. The chief secondary female character, Julia, is never introduced and one must work out by guess and context her relationship, as some sort of guardian to the main subject Margaret, an orphan, who eventually marries a German and goes to live in Germany. Margaret's relationship with her dominant and aristocratic husband breaks down. She rebels and he divorces her. She returns to England with Julia, and later finds true love and happiness with a doctor (who comes to attend the dying Julia in a rather melodramatic episode) and who is not deterred by Margaret's shame at being a divorcee.

Pfeiffer's own marriage appears to have been happy[13] and certainly she was devastated when her husband died, but she probably draws on first-hand experience of the problems of living as a wife in an alien culture, and possibly the stresses and adjustments of her early years.

There is one long passage in which the central character attempts to understand and express something of the complexities of the breakdown of her love for her husband, and the mistaken expectations and assumptions in their relationship. She explores the process by which one person, in attempting to possess the other, forces him or her, often sadly and reluctantly, to create ever higher barriers and find greater need of evasion:

> It was the binding net-work of that will
>   Which seem'd to over rule me from the first,
> And had kept ever working, close, and still,
>   While I had slept. Rudely I strove to burst
>   Its meshes, for I had a frantic thirst
> For freedom:—the poor clay he could command,
> He held—I pass'd—and left it in his hand.

---

[13] Her husband, Jürgen Edward Pfeiffer, was deeply involved with and completely supportive of her interests, especially in regard to those which were called at that time, "the emancipation of women". See his will, *Somerset House*, and a letter to Gladstone 25 March 1878, *Department of Manuscripts, British Library, London*.

And so he ruled its motion, and ordaining
  Its comings and its goings, and feigned smiles,
He was content, and thought that he was reigning
  Supreme within a round of twenty miles;
  While far beyond his realm my soul defiles,
I leave him lordship over the dull clay
To set it up, and move it as he may.

And this because when it, in early days,
  Had been informed by my own heart and mind,
He had pursued it with the ceaseless gaze
  Of inquisition, striving still to find
  An end in each light act, and to unwind
Some fancied thread of mystery, which bound
All that he could not reach, or had not found.

* * *

Let me be just; and if my thoughts are free,
  Let them be not unkind; I wrong'd him more,
And tried him more, perhaps, than he tried me.
  For he did love me in those days, and wore
  Me nearer as I think to his heart's core
Than ought beside. It was my grief and sin
To hold from him the heart he could not win.[14]

There is an eventual confrontation and then the following powerful stanzas:

>   ...he grew
> Still more enamoured as I turn'd and threw
> His menace back—for, like a tyrant, he
> Had a strange love and fear of all things free.
>
> Stung by oppression, sudden I had grown
>   What nature never meant that I should be,
> A creature wild and fierce, a panther, known
>   For its dread beauty; had it flatter'd me
>   To daunt him, and to make him bow the knee,

---

[14] Pfeiffer, *Margaret; or, The Motherless* (London, 1861) pp. 45, 46, 47.

I could have done it then, and, in his name,
Left deeds which future time might praise or blame.[15]

Later passages assert the need for women to find a valid basis for life, both emotional and practical, if necessary, without dependence on a man:

But the time is come when the Battle of Life
  Must be fought by woman, and often alone.
Many a woman can never be wife,
  And many a mother's heart makes moan
  Over the children she has never known.
Yet one thought raises her out of the dust,
  And vindicates toil in its utmost need;
One thought sweetens her slumber and crust,
  And she follows that one where the bravest lead,—
To possess herself, is her dear-bought mead.

To be self-dependent,—to spread your leaves,
  Your branches, and haply some modest flower,
Round and about you, as each receives
  A bidding from sunshine, dew or shower;
  Not to be forc'd down to trail or cower
Against the sap, away from the sun,
  At the will of another, whose narrow thought
Conceives no measure for you but his own...[16]

The statement is remarkably explicit for the 1860s. As poetry, the imagery of the tree is effective, and the verse vigorous with striking lines.[17]

---

[15] Ibid. pp. 51, 52.
[16] Ibid. pp. 92, 93.
[17] *Margaret* was published when she was 34 and is her first book of poetry. Not only is it not mentioned in the *DNB* entry, the author of which had apparently at least some personal knowledge of her or those near to her, but it is not listed among previous publications in subsequent books, although the still earlier prose romance, *Valisneria* usually is. Did she herself view it as flawed? Was she uneasy about some of its expression? Even Hickok dismisses the poem, speaking of the later book of 1873 as "Her first serious publication..." Japp also does not mention it.

IV.

Of the shorter poems, 'The Witch's Last Ride' is an interesting attempt to write something in the style of the Scottish and English traditional ballads. Unfortunately, there is a frequent use of words such as "eftsoon" "ohone" and "hist" which are difficult to hear as anything other than affectations which detract from, rather than contribute to, the tone they are meant to sustain. However, making the effort to ignore these, a mannerism of her era, the poem reads remarkably well aloud, particularly with the use of an internal rhyme in the first line and then no rhyme for the third.

> Oh it was rare, high up in air,
>   To shoot from out the drift,
> Or with a gossip cheek by jowl
>   To spin across the lift;
>
> With but one word to turn to curd
>   The nursing-mother's milk,
> And make a weanling's bones to wind
>   About your thumbs like silk;
>
> To know that lambs behind their dams
>   Would sicken as you pass;
> To poison all the earring wheat
>   And blight the meadow-grass![18]

The theme is also interesting, presented from the witch's point of view, as she realises that she has grown old and frail, even fearful of falling off her broomstick, and has only one last night ride to make. Eventually she confronts her own death and unknown terrors (or are they terrors?) ahead. There is an effective ambiguity at the end. In her final delirium, the witch imagines that her cat is some long lost child again at her breast. The pathos does not obtrude; rather it contributes to what is a poem of liberation, exaltation, even power, with a sense of the speaker being set apart from ordinary life, enjoying the camaraderie

---

[18] Pfeiffer, *Flowers of the Night* (London, 1889) pp. 10, 11.

of other witches. Even the mischief, the malevolence, the gratuitous destruction, becomes something nearer to a positive energy, an assertion of vitality otherwise excluded from the safety of the everyday.

A few of the 33 stanzas are repetitious, and in some, the rhyming of the first two half lines falters. It is nonetheless surprising that the poem has not been included in some anthology: either for dramatic recitation, or for children, or even as a feminist text. I suspect that contemporary taste may have been uneasy about its expression while later generations may have been alienated by aspects of her diction, conventional to the 1880s.

V.

There is a large number of assorted lyrics and short dramatic poems, including a few in Scots, two of which, 'A Confession' and 'The Sonsy Milk Maid'[19], have an authentic quality. Some of the lyrics probably show the influence of Heine. The best of these are 'In the Riviera'[20] and one, untitled except for 'Poem', which has an effectively enigmatic quality, unusual for her, as if a fragment of something else, or the envoi to an untold story. The unexpected and halting rhythmical effect in the last line is striking:

> June has once more brought the rose,
>   Fair beyond all praise.
> I was bold to speak in those
>   Richer bygone days.
>
> On the rose I gaze my fill,—
>   Gaze and let her be,
> Lest though I adore her still,
>   She no more know me.[21]

Pfeiffer obviously read Heine with ease in German and published some translations, with a preface that might speak for all translators: "The seemingly facile beauty of the shorter poems of Heine, and the

---

[19] Ibid. pp. 66, 68.
[20] Ibid. pp. 58, 59.
[21] Ibid. p. 60.

infinite difficulty of rendering them into our language, make of them a kind of vortex into which many translators are being unwarily drawn. I make no apology for having striven... feeling that if I am to share in the too-common lot of failure, I shall suffer it in the pursuit of a genuine object, and in company."[22]

At least two of her versions catch something of what has often been ascribed to Heine's poems in the German, that "seemingly facile beauty", casual and yet poised, passionate and yet never far from irony[23]:

> Never fear that I betray thee
>   Or our love to worldly eyes,
> Though my lips should drown thy beauty
>   Deep in metaphors and sighs.
>
> 'Neath that forest full of flowers
>   Hide discreet as in an arbour
> Every shy yet ardent secret,—
>   Every deep and secret ardour.
>
> If a tell-tale spark should flicker
>   From the rose—so let it be!
> This cold world that knows not passion
>   Takes it all for poesie.[24]

The other poem, which achieves this quality, and Heine's characteristic balance between banter and heartbreak, is even shorter:

> The letter that you sent me
>   Will do our love no wrong;

---

[22] Pfeiffer, *Quarterman's Grace and other poems* (London, 1879) p. 2 of Preface.
[23] A contemporary of Pfeiffer, James Thomson (B.V.), who also translated Heine, remarked "One can never be quite sure with Heine, and I believe that he could not be quite sure himself, where the seriousness ends and the humouristic irony begins." Quoted from an article 'Heinrich Heine' in the *Secularist* (29/1/76), by Tom Leonard *Places of the Mind* (London 1993) p. 113, from Schafer, *Selected Prose of James Thomson* (Berkeley and Los Angeles 1967) p. 258.
[24] *Quarterman's Grace*, p. 129. Whether the pattern of "arbour" "ardent" "ardour" is successful I would query, finding the effect almost more of a tongue-twister than something of melodic interest. On the other hand, the technical effect, once one makes the effort to enunciate the syllables, is striking. There is ample evidence that Pfeiffer worked her poems very carefully and that every effect of this kind is deliberately measured.

> To take back that you lent me,—
>   Your letter though is long.
>
> Twelve close and dainty pages!
>   A manuscript indeed!
> One simpler means engages
>   If but to say "God Speed."[25]

Gwyn Jones chooses to represent Pfeiffer in his anthology with one of her 'Songs': 'A Song for Winter'. I think it shows her at her most derivative, in the tradition of addressing flowers as though they had moral or human qualities.

> Barbed blossom of the guarded gorse
>   I love thee where I see thee shine:
> Thou sweetener of our common-ways,
> And brightener of our wintery days.
>
> Flower of the gorse, the rose is dead.
>   Thou art undying, O be mine!
> Be mine with all thy thorns, and prest
> Close on a heart that asks not rest.[26]

There are six more stanzas which repeat the same sentiments in language which lacks conviction.

VI.

Kathleen Hickok does not draw attention to 'Outlawed: A rhyme for the time', which is surprising, as it is the most explicit and topical of Pfeiffer's poems concerning women's issues. The occasion for its composition was a debate in the House of Commons dealing with the rights of parents over the care of their children in cases where there was dispute or separation, and giving the inevitable priority of authority to

---

[25] Ibid. p. 135
[26] Ibid. p. 97

the man.[27] Perhaps it is slightly longer than it can sustain, but the pace and rhyme is skilfully varied, managing an effective balance between light verse, even ironic fun, and passionate anger, making its points with a sarcasm which is never out of control. It is again surprising that it has not (so far as I have been able to trace) been reprinted, not just in an anthology of feminist poetry, but in one of general political and social satire. In the following extract "they" are the all male members of the House of Commons, apparently for once united in their opinion!

> This is no frivolous matter,—a topic
> Which touches them nearer than the Tropic,—
> Nearer than houses, dearer than lands;
> Here are their little ones thrown on their hands
> To guard from the ravage or [of?] something most savage;
> To save from some truculent claimant that stands
> And faces the man with its shameless demands;
> > That has crouched by the hearth
> > And sprung up on the path,
> That would suddenly open its reptile jaws,
> That would stealthily seize in its cat-like claws;
> Some lurking evil, some hooded snake
> That watches the hour and the moment to slake
> Its wrath on the man and his motherless brood
> Having no part in either. I stood,
> I waited, I watched as they took up the word,
> And deemed it some tale of romance that I heard,—
> > Some olden story
> > Of dragon hoary,—
> Of fabulous monster that over-bold
> Had come from bespoiling the lambs in the fold
> > To threaten the lambs with the tender blue eyes,
> The tearful blue eyes and the fleeces of gold;
> > But I saw that the speakers believed in their cries,
> Were sure that some monster was lying in wait

---

[27] She has this note to the poem: "See March 27, 1884 [Hansard]. Debate on Mr. Bryce's Infants' Bill, in the course of which it was made clear that the House generally regarded children as having but one parent; that one, not the woman to whose guardianship children are primarily committed by nature, but the man who frames the law by which the case between the parents, when it arises, is adjudged." *Flowers of the Night*, p. 72

More Words

> For the children of men, and were keen to abate
>   Of this power perverse the inordinate claim—
>   To hush and to crush and expose it to shame,
> Or to bone it, and render invertebrate.
>
> What is this terror, this name of fear
> That they shun to pronounce, that I tremble to hear?
> The name of this vampire that fastens and thrives
> On the tender young lives
> Of the children,—this foe whose mere shadow appals,-
>
> The name of this Spoiler for justice that calls,
>   And that justice, as such, has no choice but to smother,
> To stamp out the life of, or build up the walls?—
>   God comfort the children—this fiend IS—their MOTHER![28]

VII.

This leaves the other main area of her poetry: the sonnets, which Pfeiffer published at intervals throughout her life. They were collected together in 1880, and in a larger edition in 1886, and are technically very accomplished. The author of the entry in the *DNB* comments: "She succeeds best in the sonnet, where the metrical form enforces compression". An anonymous contemporary reviewer in America remarked "For condensation of thought, imaginative force, and fine artistic sense, it would be hard to equal some of [them]".[29]

Most are rather dated now, in their preoccupation with idealised romantic love, and great use of abstractions with initial capital letters resulting in lines such as:

> Weird Nature! can it be that joy is fled,
>   And bald unmeaning lurks beneath thy smile?
>   That beauty haunts the dust but to beguile,
> And that with Order, Love and Hope are dead?[30]

---

[28] Ibid. pp. 72–89.
[29] *Boston Daily Advertiser*. Quoted at back of *Flowers of the Night*.
[30] Pfeiffer, *Sonnets and Songs* (London, 1880) p. 7.

Many other forgotten, as well as better known contemporaries of Pfeiffer, wrote equally skilful, if unremarkable, exercises in the genre.[31] However, it is those few which transcend the conventions of the time which are worth remarking. I would submit that Pfeiffer did achieve a handful which deserve to stand with the best of her contemporaries and immediate predecessors without apology.

The lines quoted above come from the first of four sonnets entitled 'To Nature' which as a group build up to some memorable passages:

> Dull fount of joy, unhallowed source of tears,
>   Cold motor of our fervid faith and song,
> Dead, but engendering life, love, pangs, and fears,
>   Thou crownedst thy wild work with foulest wrong
> When first thou lightedst on a seeming goal
> And darkly blundered on man's suffering soul.[32]

The final sonnet of this sequence, with its arresting last line, reads:

> If we be fools of chance, indeed, and tend
>   No whither, then the blinder fools in this:
>   That, loving good, we live, in scorn of bliss,
> Its wageless servants to the evil end.
> If, at the last, man's thirst for higher things
>   Be quenched in dust, the giver of his life,
>   Why press with growing zeal a hopeless strife,—
> Why—born for creeping—should he dream of wings?
> O Mother Dust! thou hast one law so mild
>   We call it sacred—all thy creatures own it—
> The tie which binds the parent and the child,—
>   Why has man's loving heart alone outgrown it?
> Why hast thou travailed so to be denied,
> So trampled by a would-be matricide?[33]

---

[31] Another contemporary comments: "Her sonnets are thoughtful and intelligible, in this wise differing from the work of many sonnet-mongers [although] in her more arduous flights she often fails…" E.C. Stedman, *Victorian Poets* (London, 1887) pp. 453–454.
[32] *Sonnets and Songs*, p. 8.
[33] Ibid. p. 10.

There are at least two sonnets which give effective expression to direct personal experience. One of these is 'A Reminiscence'[34] where the poignancy of a childhood memory is not lost in sentimentality. The other is 'Among the Hebrides' which has the advantage of escaping, for once, from the iambic pentameter:

> From blue Loch Carron rise white and sheer
>   Its bare rock faces and island cones,
>   And they glitter as frost and wind-bleached bones;
> Coral and sapphire far and near,
> Pearl-white coral and sapphire clear,
>   Finely-chiselled as cameo stones,
>   No blurred edges or soft mixed tones;
> Blue as the bottomless, white as fear.
> Do I sleep, do I dream, in the hard clear day,
>   On the windy deck, in the afternoon,
> With the sough of the wave, and the spume of the spray,
>   And my hair like the dank sea-tangle blown
> On the landward breeze? Is it Portree bay
>   That we make, or some cove in the long-dead moon?[35]

The pattern of sound and sustained rhyme reinforces the imagery; and I find the repetition, always a risky device, of lines 4–5, convincing. Line 8 is particularly incisive, and the final image of line 14.

Her sonnet on the death of George Eliot, although commented on favourably elsewhere,[36] is not, in my view, very successful; but the first of two entitled 'On Hearing the Introduction to *Lohengrin*'[37] is striking.

The sonnets of Pfeiffer worth particular attention are a group of four entitled 'Studies from the Antique', two on Kassandra and two on Klytemnestra, first published in the *Contemporary Review* for 1878.[38]

---

[34] Pfeiffer, *Under the Aspens* (London, 1882) p. 14
[35] *Sonnets and Songs*, p. 34.
[36] Stedman singles out (with the one on Shelley) the sonnet on George Eliot for particular praise as does Hickok but I wonder whether it is chiefly ideological sympathy with the subject matter which attracts them.
[37] *Sonnets and Songs* p. 19.
[38] *Contemporary Review* (London, June 1878) Volume XXXII, pp. 455,456.

There are many Greek heroines whom Pfeiffer might have chosen with attributes nearer to what was conventionally expected of, or admired in women in the 1870s. It is difficult to imagine that these two were a random choice, or assigned to her on commission; but however arrived at or however conscious she was of all the implications, it is probable, that by using the mask of 'Studies from the Antique' she was able to free herself to express things absent from most of her other poems, and in a concomitantly more vigorous manner. By framing them as 'Studies', they are distanced slightly from her, as for example, the sonnet addressed to George Eliot is not.

One of the strongest of this group of four is the first of the two to 'Kassandra':

> Virgin of Troy, the days were well with thee
>   When wandering singing by the singing streams
>   Of Ilion, thou beheldest the golden gleams
> Of the bold sun that might not faced be,
> Come murmuring to thy feet caressingly;
>   But best that day when, steeped in noontide dreams,
>   The young Apollo wrapped thee in his beams,
> And quenched his love in thine as in a sea!
> And later, in thy tower 'twas sweet to teach
>   The loveless night the joys high day had known;
> To dream, to wake—and find thy love impeach
>   Late sleep with kisses, and thy spirit flown
> To his, and at the ivory gates of speech
>   Breaking in words as burning as his own.[39]

The technical virtuosity of the rhymes never intrudes but impels the text forward and there is the power of phrases such as "quenched his love in thine", "impeach late sleep with kisses" and "the ivory gates of speech / breaking in words". The central imagery of the sun, which could be "quenched" only in the "sea" of Kassandra's love, is well sustained, and expresses a sensuality which may have been more than she realised. The last line is particularly effective. One might speculate on the problems that must have faced her, writing on subjects such as this in the 1870s.

The most powerful poem in the sequence is one of the two to 'Klytemnestra':

---

[39] *Sonnets and Songs* p. 45.

> Daughter of gods and men, great ruling will,
>   Seething in oily rage within the sphere
>   Which gods and men assign the woman here,
> Till, stricken where the wound approved thee still
> Mother and mortal, all the tide of ill
>   Rushed through the gap, and nothing more seemed dear
>   But power to wreck high ruin, nothing clear
> But the long dream you waited to fulfil.
> Mother and spouse—queen of the king of men—
>   What fury brought Aegysthus to thy side?—
> That bearded semblant, man to outward ken,
>   Or else mere mawworm, made to fret man's pride;
> Woman, thy foot was on thy tyrant then—
> Mother, thou wert avenged for love defied![40]

Most of the poem is fairly explicit, and directly based on the classical story of Klytemnestra's revenge, but there are also other meanings, less easily defined. There is the vigour of phrases such as "great ruling will", "seething in oily rage", "all the tide of ill", "that bearded semblant", "to fret man's pride" and "avenged for love defied" as well as the imagery of "the wound" or "gap" through which "rushed through" that "power to wreck high ruin", with a more general range of associations linked to female sexuality in "the tide" rushing through "the wound".

If there is no direct syntactical linking of "the wound" of line 4 and "gap" of line 6 with "the sphere" assigned to "woman", in the context of the poem, it can be implied. The syntax of "the wound approved thee still/ mother and mortal" is clear but there is something additional which is "stricken" into or through that "wound" or "gap". A double hurt is thus suggested; perhaps both Klytemnestra's generally assigned "sphere" as woman—also "daughter", "mother", "spouse"—and the particular injury or oppression by "[her] tyrant"?

The use of "defied" is of course conditioned by the rhyme scheme, but this not merely accidental as another sequence could have been found, and the rhyme emphasises the choice. Defiance thus becomes a fitting climax to the poem, and her retribution for that "love defied"; in this case, the defiance by Iphigenia's father of a mother's love which Klytemnestra was avenging.

---

[40] Ibid. p. 47.

If we may wish she had written more "words as burning" as these, I would submit that few poets may be so fortunate as to have written so many.

Some Afterwords

A poem, once made, must speak for itself. The hopes, ideas, difficulties or circumstances of its maker may be of curiosity but are in the end, irrelevant.

Most persons, however, are curious about other people and in our response to a poem we often experience, even intensely, something that is akin to what is called in other contexts *personality*. There is the understandable conviction that this sense of a person speaking to us in the poem must have connection with the person who assembled the words.

Yet other experience tells us that this connection is not straightforward, that a poem in which we may take delight or find engaging, may be written by someone we find unpleasant or even tedious. And there is the sense in which all poems are fictions, even when the "I" of the poem may appear to be that of the maker. Thus what a writer may say about his connection with what he has written needs to be read with caution.

*

I am aware of a lack of consistency over the course of time in regard to my own ideas about the construction of poems, even, in the words of the Catechism, of that "chief end". Some were written for my own interest, at least initially. Others specifically for a public context. Others to complement set rhythms or patterns, or were constructed from or upon the words of other men or women. Some are based on single images, some on the relationships of a multiplicity. Some, which I would not wish to disown, jests and ballads, are more appropriate to the spoken occasion than the printed page. Some, now mostly fallen away, were written in the mistaken notion that I might impress or inform the world.

I have often had the wish that I might have been born into another age and had the fortune to be court poet, makar or skald, to a minor chief or lord, called upon to provide poems for particular occasions, to celebrate, to mourn, even to castigate or to jest, finding voice for public and private experience, in a context which could be defined. What context there is for a poet today, at least in what is known as "the

Some Afterwords

West", seems mostly bound up with the words *literature* and *culture*, much annexed by universities and Arts Councils. Committees decide who shall receive grants, examination papers are even set and there are obviously those who are able to relate their poems to such a context.

There is also the point of view expressed by a recent commentator: "…that every poet's task is ultimately and essentially, if not mythopoeic, at any rate religious; and that it is dangerous for any poet to think otherwise." We must make our choices as best we can.

*

I have in the past committed to print, sometimes rashly in retrospect, and to notebooks for my own use, various speculations as to what I thought poetry, even my own, was *about*. A few quotations may give a background of intention if not always of result, which may be of curiosity and can be ignored if not.

"…the form of a poem must be of positive use—and it may be that it functions more in the making than in the result… Where certain words, or in certain places, are 'given' then the final result is not entirely dependent on our choice, except of that initial design… The free form suggests nothing… it is a much harder form in which to write something that is verbally and conceptually interesting."

"…the most rigorous distinction between Fancy and Imagination… between Fable and Vision, need not deny that one may open upon the other."

"Recurrence, Resonance, Reassertion, Refrain—yet with Variety, Variation—these are all words that carry something of what makes verse characteristic—the mind takes pleasure in these… 'To get into the rhythm of something'… is to get into harmony with it—these are also terms to do with the activity of living our lives—so equally they are terms we use in thinking about poetry and its structure."

"…in writing [a poem]…when we speak of something, we affect it. The very language we use is not *mine* but only *ours*… as what is said is shaped by meanings which are in the pattern… which perhaps we discover as much as create."

"…clarity and concision; but these are dead without cogency, and it is the cogency of an individual in a living situation which provides the greatest urgency. I would like to write poems which combine astonishment that a poem should be so, with astonishment that anyone might suppose that it could be otherwise."

From an appreciation of another poet: "…many pleasures, but chiefly these: the conviction of direct knowledge of physical experience and: an unfailing devotion to the poem as a construction of words to be both said and heard."

"…many sorts of interest which a poem may have but without an essential grain of delight in language and in the possibilities of utterance, I believe that it [the writing and reading] is all in vain."

Sources

p.11 An Autobiographical Sketch
Northward Journal 50-51, 1990.

p.15 Charlotte Chapel
PN Review 28, 1982.

p.21 A Letter from Canada
Chanticleer 1:4, Spring 1954.

p.24 Migrant — A Personal Account
Credences (Buffalo) 1981/82.

p.27 An Announcement
Leaflet prepared 1957.

p29 Dancing for an Hour
Chapman 78-79, 1994.

p.41 Then is Now
Scripsi (Melbourne) 3:2, August 1985.

p.44 A Visit to Basil Bunting
From the author's notebooks, dated by him Winter 1964/65. Transcribed by Jill Turnbull.

p.53 An Arlespenny
King Ida's Watch Chain, Link One, 1965.

p.61 The Poet as Makar
The Star You Steer By: Basil Bunting and British Modernism, ed. James McGonigal & Richard Price (Amsterdam: Rodopi, 2000).

p.63 The Spoils
Marked 'Compost' by the author.

p.65 Bunting, Brigflatts and Margaret Greenbank
A typescript by the author was discovered, after his death, in a folder containing his correspondence with Bunting. It seems to have been intended to be held back until all after the deaths of all involved.

p.77 A Visit to William Carlos Williams
The Massachusetts Review Winter 1962.

p.82 A Gesture to be Clean
Satis 2, Spring 1961.

p.93 From a Notebook
Published, but it is unclear from the author's records where this occurred.

p.95 Il Miglior fabbro
Found on the author's word processor.

p.97 Some Notes on *The Maximus Poems*
Combustion 5, January 1958.

p.100 Cid Corman
Found on the author's word processor. It is unclear whether this was ever published, but it dates from the mid-1960s.

p.103 Some Notes on the Poetry of Robert Duncan
New Measure 6, Summer 1967.

p.109 From a Journal (Ginsberg)
Taken from the author's journals, dated 9 February 1958. Transcribed by Jill Turnbull.

p.111 Paris and Bill Burroughs
Mica 5, Winter 1962.

p.115 Laura Riding: First Awakenings
Lines Review 122, September 1992.

p.118 The *Selected Poems* of Raymond Souster
Sparrow 6, November 1956.

p.120 Saint-Denys-Garneau
Southfields 4:1, 1997.

p.127 What is Poetry *About?*
Dated 1990. Found on the author's word processor.

Sources

p.138 Identity and Ideology
    Found on the author's word processor.

p.142 Resonances and Speculations
    Kulchur 2:7, Autumn 1962.

p.149 Some Notes on *The Ship's Orchestra*
    Grosseteste Review 1:2, Autumn 1972.

p.152 Edinburgh May 1963 — Ian Hamilton Finlay
    Found on the author's word processor.

p.163 Letter
    The English Intelligencer, Cambridge 1966. Series 1, Issue 3, edited by Andrew Crozier. Thanks to Ian Brinton for providing a copy of this item.

p.165 *Arabic and Persian Poems*
    Agenda 9:2-3, Spring-Summer 1971.

p.168 Hugh Creighton Hill's *A Soundproof Gesture*
    A Migrant Press flier advertising a publication in August 1982.

p.170 A Letter to Sylvia Turner
    Found on the author's word processor.

p.173 William Price Turner: An Appreciation
    Poetry Review 89:2, Summer 1999.

p.176 John Adlard
    Written for a memorial volume which never appeared.

p.181 Remarks on Some Poems by Emily Pfeiffer
    Paper given at the *Rethinking Women's Poetry* conference at Birkbeck, University of London, in 1995. It has not previously been published.

p.198 Some Afterwords
    from Gael Turnbull, *While Breath Persists: New and Selected Poems* (Erin, ONT: The Porcupine's Quill Inc. 1991).

www.ingramcontent.com/pod-product-compliance
Lightning Source LLC
Chambersburg PA
CBHW022008160426
43197CB00007B/340